C000262114

LETTERS FROM ALDEBURGH

Letters from Aldeburgh

Joyce Grenfell

Edited by Janie Hampton

Day Books

ISBN 10: 0953 2213 7 7

ISBN 13: 978 0953 2213 7 0

A catalogue record for this book is available from the British Library

First published by Day Books, June 2006

Printed in the United Kingdom by the Alden Press. This publication is printed on acid-free paper

Day Books, Orchard Piece, Crawborough, Charlbury,
Oxfordshire OX7 3TX, UK

www.day-books.com

To my mother Verily
who became engaged to my step-father Paul Paget
during a concert at the Maltings on 5 June 1971.
Peter Pears was singing Schumann's *Winterreise*,
accompanied by Benjamin Britten on the piano.
Joyce and Reggie Grenfell were sitting a few seats away.

Introduction

THE WRITER AND ENTERTAINER JOYCE GRENFELL is best known for her monologues and her cameo roles in the St Trinian's films. Less well known is her love of the small town of Aldeburgh in Suffolk, a love which combined three of her greatest preoccupations – music, birds and friends.

Joyce's favourite form of creative expression was music. She would rather go to a concert than to the theatre, cinema or an exhibition. She liked 'all types of music, as long as it is good' and this encompassed Bach, Beethoven, Britten, Gershwin and Richard Rodgers. She preferred chamber music to symphonies, and could not bear 'hill-billy twanging' or organs with 'vox humana' pipes.

Joyce first began to enjoy music as a schoolgirl, when her father took her to the Proms at the Queen's Hall in Regent's Street. For some reason she believed at the time that it was essential to wear a blue aertex shirt while listening to 'important' music. She later wrote,

> When I was young I listened because I saw pictures or liked the rhythms. Certain music stirred me, made me cry, yearn, sigh, gloat and wallow. I stood night after night at the Proms emoting and getting nourished. Later I began to hear what I was listening to, and the wallowing decreased, while the nourishment increased.

As a young woman during the Second World War, she attended the lunchtime concerts at the National Gallery organised by Myra Hess. She never claimed to be a music critic, but throughout her working life she listened to a great deal of it, not only at concerts but on gramophone records and the Third Programme. After her retirement from the stage, her role in the BBC television programme 'Face the Music' demonstrated the wide knowledge she had acquired. Hers was always a very personal appreciation: unlike other music-lovers, she noted in her letters and diaries what a musician was wearing, and what the weather was doing outside during a performance.

Aldeburgh is a fishing town, largely unchanged since its heyday in the early 19th century. The High Street is lined with original shops, and the fishermen's cottages are painted in a charming variety of colours. Benjamin Britten and Peter Pears established the Music Festival there in 1948. Britten believed passionately in his East Anglian roots and in his duty to serve the community. He wrote:

> I have tried to bring music to Aldeburgh in the shape of our local Festival; and all the music I write comes from it.

The Festival became one of the most successful in the country, mainly because the local community was involved. The Cranbrook children for example, from a local family, played leading parts in Britten's opera *The Little Sweep*; and pilots at the nearby US Air Force base agreed not to fly their jets overhead during the concerts.

In the early days, festival events took place in the Jubilee Hall, the Parish Church, the Baptist Chapel, on the sea front and in the half-timbered High Street cinema. The three-week programme of two or three concerts a day gave both audience and participants plenty of time to digest the music and enjoy leisurely meals. As Bernard Levin wrote:

> The quality of the Aldeburgh Festival is not so much a series of performances as a gathering of friends – on both sides of the footlights. The performances are of the very highest standard, but everybody seems to be doing it for fun.

Joyce Grenfell was first introduced to the festival in 1962 by her friend and colleague, the pianist Viola Tunnard. Viola had travelled with her around the Middle East and India during the Second World War, entertaining the troops. Although Viola had accompanied Joyce in her repertoire of popular songs, she preferred to be known as a classical pianist. After the war she was increasingly in demand as a rehearsal pianist for opera and ballet, and was both a versatile player and an accomplished musician. Viola was a devoted member of Britten's musical team, working with Janet Baker and Peter Pears and performing duets with Britten himself.

Although she performed her songs and monologues at four festivals, Joyce really felt that she was part of the audience, and in the list of Festival Subscribers she modestly called herself 'Mrs R. Grenfell'. Each year she wrote to Britten after the festival, exclaiming that it was 'the Best Ever!'

It was not only the music that the Grenfells loved about Aldeburgh. The festival was held in June, when the countryside was bursting with fresh green growth and flowers. When they weren't attending concerts, Joyce and her husband Reggie would set off armed with sandwiches, notebooks and binoculars. Although Reggie usually drove the car, it was Joyce who set the pace.

'We like to drive slowly,' she said. 'Then we can see the flowers.'

'So damn slowly,' Reggie murmured, 'that we can see them growing.'

One day they identified twenty-one different species flowering on Aldeburgh beach.

Suffolk was also ideal for bird-watching. Joyce watched birds the same way that she watched people – quietly, unobserved, taking mental notes and sometimes sketching them. She discovered that bird-watching was the perfect antidote to fame and a busy life, and if fellow 'twitchers' recognised her, they rarely mentioned it. The Maltings concert hall sits beside Snape Marsh, a muddy estuary where over a hundred species of birds breed each year. When, in 1969, the sea broke through and flooded the land right up to Snape, putting the delicate flora and fauna at risk of permanent damage, Reggie helped to raise the £8,000 needed to restore the sea wall.

Nine miles along the coast from Aldeburgh is Minsmere Bird Reserve where Herbert Axell, the Warden, masterminded the world's first man-made lagoon for birds. Minsmere was his kingdom and he expected visitors to respect his birds, which included marsh harriers, avocets, bearded tits, long-eared owls and bitterns with their booming fog-horn call. He wrote:

At Minsmere one goes at one's own pace for a few hundred yards or the full four miles. You keep to the paths on which birds have become accustomed to seeing people move and you do not run; and the flowers are not for you to pick – you can paint them if you wish. When Joyce and Reggie visit the reserve she often stays behind in a hide to sketch while we go on. A glorious day on the marsh has sometimes been too much for Joyce's joie de vivre, causing her to break forth into song.

When Herbert retired, the Grenfells bought him and his wife a cottage near Minsmere. Although they toyed with the idea of buying a holiday cottage of their own in the town, they decided that they preferred the freedom and sociability of a hotel. They usually stayed in the Wentworth, at the north end of the promenade, where Joyce often plunged into the North Sea, leaving Reggie to guard her towel. Reggie rarely swam – even in tropical waters he tended to turn blue.

After their first introduction to Aldeburgh, the Grenfells were hooked and they came back for the next seventeen years. Every day of each festival, Joyce wrote to her friend Virginia Graham, describing what was going on in vivid detail. These letters, together with her correspondence with Benjamin Britten, are presented here as a tribute to Aldeburgh and its festival.

Janie Hampton

1962

Wentworth Hotel, Aldeburgh, Suffolk
16 June 1962

Darling Virginia,

We meandered down yesterday through the most rural bits of Suffolk. We came via Chigwell, the Rosings, Sudbury, and never touched a big town or main road. Singularly few flowers about but England very green and pleasant.

I do love this Festival and this hotel. *Everyone* is concerned in the goings on and there is the sea and yesterday the sun shone.

The Amadeus Quartet last night in the packed church. Reggie says he liked it too. The slow movement of the Mozart was best. Viola joined us after and then she and I went back to the church for the Deller Consort doing very early Flemish music. Ooh such sonorous tones. Marvellous squeezed harmonies and cool soaring sounds rising out of richness. I thought it marvellous. The church floodlit, a moon and a warm night to walk in.

Saw Nina, Bill and Bronwen Astor, Puffin Asquith, Lady Dashwood and Dorothy Chamberlain who I went to school with in 1922. Also B. Britten and P. Pears and of course glorious Imogen Holst.

Much love, Joyce.

Life here is delicious. Weather has been good and there is sun and cloud today and a breeze too. Yesterday, wearing twelve-year-old trousers and feeling a proper Charley in them, we collected victuals from a grocery and drove to Orford Quay to join the birding launch. Such a funny lot.

One old man of 83, who was immobile as a tree, had to be lowered to the boat. He was, I fancy, an ex-Judge or QC. He and an elderly Jewish gent exchanged legal gossip in the boat and their elderly wives carried picnic bags.

There were two youngish women, possibly teachers, unsuitably clad in vivid cottons, white 'cardies', plastic macs and thin shoes; a trio of open-air middle-agers, and a Mrs Bridgeman in windcheater and tiny sailing hat that looked glued on. I would have put her down instantly as bridge club, golf club, and not at all my dish. But not a bit of it, turned out to be very nice and *very* knowledgeable. Not only was she bird mad but sailing crazy, and spends time voluntarily teaching the young to sail under a Government Scheme for Physical Education. She was amusing and unlikely. Last year she attended a bird-song course in Yorkshire, costing seven guineas all in, sleeping in a cubicle and walking five miles a day. She said it was enormously unexpected and her husband thought her mad, but advised us to go and we are seriously contemplating it.

We saw nothing but sky above pale bending reeds, and bearded tits and beautiful giddy-coloured redstarts. You know avocets don't you? Lots of baby avocets, also godwits and teal and a short-eared owl to divert us.

Last night *Dido* most beautifully sung. Today is Blythburgh and some *Tchaikovsky!* Tonight harpsichords in the parish church. Reggie is bearing up well.

Walking along the front, we came on Hans Keller, the musicologist, and his artist wife in a state of panic – they had no transport and he *had* to be at Blythburgh to supervise the concert, being broadcast by BBC. So we drove them over, taking a picnic with us. Heavenly church: full of light it was, and radiant. Lovely concert. Tchaikovsky and Mozart – interestingly unexpected mixture.

Later to the parish church for harpsichords and unaccompanied flute. This was testing for Reggie but he survived. Elizabeth Lutyens flute piece was alarming; and double Bach was glorious but too fast. Ridiculously fast. Rattly and *silly*. Full moon on the sea.

Nobly I think I must give up the morning Debussy I crave and go early with R. to Minsmere for birds.

19 June 1962

We were so energetic yesterday – a heavenly day of sun and breeze and we left our extra wool in the car. An unescorted day at Minsmere, but from time to time we coincided in hides, and that was useful because experts told us what they'd seen and it helped us beginners.

Lovely lute concert last night at Thorpeness. Julian Bream, with little pieces with funny names. One was 15th century and called 'Carman's whistle'. R. loved it.

Full moon barred by black clouds and it looked a bit menacing.

20 June 1962

Another nature day. Today lunch in a field *carpeted* in viper's-bugloss, pink Herb Robert, yellow mustard, wild mignonettes, bladder campion, speedwell *and* yellow calves'-foot. It was a sight and a joy, and it also contained a lot of greedy linnets and a pair of hares.

Then the opera school gave Mozart's one-acter *The Impresario*. It's a ravishing piece and they did it excellently well.

Then later Curzon, Britten and Pears in a prog. of Schumann and the big piano fantasy (which I can't abide – German guff and wallow and total absence of real heart.) Then a lot of Debussy songs and duets, four hands on one piano. P.P. sang well, but it takes more than two great stars to make good *duetting*, and the tangle of huge hands avoiding each other, pretty dextrously, didn't quite add up to a performance.

21 June 1962

The English food is very good here – well cooked and changeable if you get my meaning. There *is* fruit salad and 'coupes' but also castle pudding, and to R.'s pleasure, always a savoury.

Lady Listowel has vanished. Charlotte Bonham-Carter, in a turned up Breton and her hair *down* like a sixteen-year-old, drove here just for *Albert Herring* and then back to town in order to attend Lady Dashwood's ball tonight.

Herring was very enjoyable indeed, even though Sylvia Fisher is too soft and sweet for a bully Lady of the Manor. But well sung and directed and very funny.

Happy Aldeburgh to you.

Love, Joyce.

1963

Wentworth Hotel, Aldeburgh
24 June 1963

Darling Ginnie

We had a whale of a day of air and birding yesterday. *Hot* sun quite often and I'm tinged now and Reggie is bright brown. Avocets, redshank etc and back at Orford to have a cupper at the Crown, get into my suit (knitted) from my skirt (sailcloth) before a *superb* concert at the church. Best of all so far. Lennox Berkeley, Bach (Menuhin) and St Nicholas. Atmospheric and satisfying. Viola was very much in evidence in the Bach and the Britten.

Earlier I saw a piece of moon come up out of the sea.

27 June 1963

Weather: mixed and only a brief little shower.

It's very difficult not to be a bore about birds but I will try. I just *must* tell you that we saw a purple heron, very very rare indeed, and we saw him long and close. Even the warden nearly exploded with excitement. We also saw a wood sandpiper, ruffs, and spotted redshank, as well as avocets.

You park your car on the lighthouse cliffs and walk a mile to the warden's hut. Our party was Mr and Mrs Rannal of Oxted and Dr Wilson of Cambridge. Our guide wore very old rain-soaked tennis-shoes, little knitted cap, zippered jacket and haversack, all of us hung with field glasses.

We sat in a row on the dunes, and saw birds of all types. As we rose to walk on we saw a dinghy-yacht in trouble about 300 yards out. Two figures in life-jackets were struggling. Suddenly over she sent. Vanished! Then the couple reappeared, clinging to the hull. Of course I was hard at it declaring the power of God. One felt, otherwise, useless. A couple of bird-watchers approached and said they'd go up to the lighthouse and telephone. I was glad not to have to watch and wait, and having decided God was better at the job, I left it to Him. About thirty minutes later a helicopter flew over and later we learned a rescue had been effected. The relief was big.

Bert Axell, the head warden, is a charmer. He is so expert and yet kind to fools. The whole thing is done very quietly and leisurely, and although one walks a hellofa long way, it is so attractive and interesting that you don't notice.

28 June 1963

Wet today. But I don't mind much. We're so full of air and sights and sounds and there are all those books we haven't even opened. And stitching. And a comfy bed to sleep on.

Yesterday was Sir Kenneth Clark's lecture on Turner, and a beauty. With slides. Full house, pin silent. Much of it was a revelation to me and very helpful towards understanding modern painting.

Last night Russian soprano Galina Vishnevskaya sang, as did Peter Pears and Mr Glossop. Operatic arias– Mozart, Verdi, Tchaikovsky. Galina has a voice of steel and total command. *Aida* and *Onegin* were thrilling but she couldn't *begin* on Mozart. Awful. Arch, rushed and bad. But oh my, the *Onegin*! Mr Glossop has a splendid voice, and of course Mr Pears is a dream Mozart singer.

The Stephen Ward case begins today. Oh dear.

Having a *nice* hol, ta.

Love Joyce.

Back in London, Joyce wrote to Britten:

> Elm Park Gardens, London
> 2 July 1963

Please may I say 'Dear Ben' because it is so unnatural to put Dear Mr Britten after hearing everyone in Aldeburgh say Ben?

Many thanks for yet another lovely and heartening festival.

The something 'special' about this festival stems from the qualities you and Peter bring to it and I think this touches some responsive spring in all of those who come close to it. That is why it is so richly satisfying and so entirely different from anywhere else in the world where they have festivals.

We came away nourished and refreshed.

Yours sincerely,

Joyce Grenfell.

When Britten invited Joyce to perform her monologues and songs the following year, Reggie responded positively:

> 15 August 1963

Dear Ben Britten

Joyce is in Australia where she has just completed her first – and triumphal – tour at Adelaide.

I am quite sure that Joyce will consider your invitation as one of the greatest compliments she could possibly receive. Because that is her opinion of the Aldeburgh festival, I am equally certain that she will delightedly say Yes, and on the day you choose. For myself, I think it is the Saturday of the Lord's Test Match against the Australians – however as I am all in favour of Aldeburgh and of Joyce – that seems a very minor entertainment. Joyce will, I know, write to you direct.

Yours sincerely,

Reggie Grenfell.

1964

When Joyce performed her songs and monologues in the Jubilee Hall, Aldeburgh, the programme stated: 'For further information about Miss Grenfell the reader is referred to Who's Who, Who's Who in America, Who's Who in Australia, Qui est Qui, Wer ist Wer (oder Was), Chi e Chi, *and probably* Kto Kto.*' After the show she wrote:*

24 June 1964

My Dear Ben

Aldeburgh is the best festival in the world and to be asked to be part of the best festival in the world gave me so much pleasure that I don't know how to say Thank you enough. It is the compliment I am prouder of than anything that has ever happened to me.

I mean this.

I must say thank you, too, to you for all your music past and present – and future. It would be impertinent to do more than say that I feel as if I had been taken into space. For space isn't just miles of emptiness (nor is Eternity) is it, but part of the whole *now*. And far more *hopeful* than we are always allowed to believe. I am very grateful to you for taking me there. I always feel music, such as Beethoven's late quartets, is already there from the beginning.

The whole festival this year has been a wonderful experience. Being allowed to do my programme in the same Festival as your music and those remarkable Russians has been very exciting for me.

Thank you so much with love Joyce.

PS Please thank Peter, too, for his singing in *Curlew River* – oh and in the Schumann – etc. etc!

Britten replied: 'It was a joy to have you here, and we are grateful to you for the incomparably funny and wise evening you gave us – we were the honoured ones! Come back again, both of you, and do another such evening for us – "as near the bone" as you like to make it. Love Ben.'

1965

Sunday 20 June 1965

Darling Virginia,

I caught the train from Liverpool Street and had a lovely sunny journey through East Anglia, rivers gleaming, sails out on wide waters near Colchester – or is it Ipswich? – eglantine in flower, poppies out, fields beginning to wave with rising corn, and everything very English and *beautiful.* I am swep' with an inner joy by it all, and there was my lover Reggie at Saxmundham, waiting at the level-crossing gates for me.

Two elderly gents came into my compartment full of the discomfort of the seats at Lord's. They boomed about their need to know how to cook. Their wives won't let them get near their stoves and then they are helpless when left alone. They have decided to get onto the local WI and arrange for lessons next winter.

Viola welcomed us and we sauntered along to the Jubilee Hall for a *most* enjoyable new version of *Let's Make an Opera.*

Yesterday we made the most of the morning with some birding and an afternoon concert with P. Pears and the Philomusica of London in a new Polish work. Fascinating. And in the evening I went to the Parish Church to hear Fishcher-Dieskau and Richter do a cycle of songs by Brahms called *Magelone*. It was superb singing and playing, but solid Brahms lies heavy on the chest: so lush, so rich, *so* many climaxes. But lovely noises made.

Earlier Lettice Coleman and Diana Albemarle (Countess of) came over and we asked them to dine with us. Lady Alb. is very pretty and sort of 'bien' which nowadays I find curiously untasteful. She was talking loudly in that upper-class voice that gets my spine shaking, totally unaware of the (mild) resentment it engenders. Richard Hoggart told me it took him ages to get over her voice, which he assumed meant arrogance, when *really* she does lots of truly good works. Perhaps it is this confidence that irritates, for she's *very* nice. She may be a tiny bit deaf, which would explain the head on one side and rather fixed eyes.

22 June 1965

Last night we went, full of suspicion, to see an Indian Temple dancer, and oh boy, were we not right! It was also hugely funny. An American woman of uncertain age with her hair in a braid, wearing a sari, announced each dance in a monotonous voice that made the whole thing even funnier for she used lots of incomprehensible Indian words too – 'the spana will dance in ecstacy to the schwarambin, in seven beats.' And bits of Sanskrit 'My lord has developed an aversion to me.' Hysteria was only just kept at bay. It went on forever. Numb bum, agonising boredom, but manners prevailed and we returned for part 2. The dancer was plump and heavy and wore a diamond in each nostril and a third dangler hanging between. Her hands were bendy and articulate, her feet were flat. She stood on one leg sometimes, jumped hard on to the stage with a heavy thump. If it had been brief it would have been enjoyably funny. But I got cross with the monotony of the music – three glum men cross-legged and a girl with a huge sort of mandolin that buzzed endlessly. One man sang in that high drone. He had a soda siphon beside him and took sips of fizzy water. Just when it was over and she'd had three bouquets, by gum back they all came, and improvised for another ten minutes.

Tomorrow Viola will play for Peter Pears, then Bream accompanies him in a new Lennox Berkeley piece for voice and guitar.

Tonight Schubert with Britten and Richter, so it's a rich feast.

A cloudburst is lashing us.

Must get up, all love and happy hols to you,

Joyce.

1966

Wentworth Hotel, Aldeburgh
10 June 1966

Darling Virginia,

Battleship grey sea with fitful gleams of sunshine. All the usuals here, such as Lady Dashwood, in modern clothes and assisted brunette hair-do. We all say 'Hello – how nice to see you' – and mean it, for a sense of continuity prevails.

Yesterday was *so* pretty that I got homesick for England and I haven't even left it yet. Every cottage garden is ablaze with roses. Some are actually *smothered*. Wild roses out just now, making Tudor patterns all over the now dark hedges, and what with them and the foaming Queen Anne's lace in the ditches and the great hanging creamy elderflower heads the whole thing is a fair treat. New corn was bending and grasses tossed about.

Unpacked and settled ourselves into the bow-windowed room on the second floor. Spacious and pleasant. Then a meander along the prom and back down the inside road and we came upon Laurens and Ingaret van der Post having tea on deck chairs in the porch of their pretty little white cottage called 'Half Crown Cottage'. So we paused briefly and planned a dinner together.

Last night was the opening of Britten's *Burning Fiery Furnace*, done in the same stylised manner as *Curlew River*. It's the story of Shadrack and his friends disobeying Nebuchadnezzar for the love of God, and it is dramatic and telling, with chanting monks processing across the stage. Lovely 'effects'. Colin Graham's direction is so inventive and imaginative and I love the way the play begins, and ends, in darkness and silence. Peter Pears is

Nebuchadnezzar and Reggie thought his very elaborate headdress, jewels and gold clothes were rather too 'camp'. But I was so relieved to find him not a pantomime dame as in *Curlew River* that I liked all the glitter. The music is fascinating and how they learned it I don't know for there is a lot of interweaving and every man for himself that can't have been easy to memorise. I know it wasn't, for Viola has been teaching the lads for months. She looks well and relaxed too.

Mr Ove Arup, who is here to build the new concert hall at Snape, is full of charm. He is currently *engineering* Sydney Opera House, trying to interpret the architect's impractical but brilliant designs.

Must get up, all love and happy hol.

11 June 1966

No sign of thunder here, but plenty of fresh air. R. and I took samwidges and parked near Minsmere Sluice and the Eel's Foot pub. I settled down after half a mile to study a willow – did two rough sketches. So *difficult*. Then we met by a bushy wood and a ditch and ate. After lunch we kipped in a lane before tea with Fidelity and Jack Cranbook of Great Glenham. Good sturdy square East Anglian house, full of *little* landscapes and vast Victorian portraits. Fidelity is nice and amusing: mother of at least six children and a dozen grands. Looks like a teenager in shape, straightish hair worn short and casual. She is a remarkable woman – *good* I suspect. Tea on lawn with the Prince and Princess of Hesse.

Lovely day ended with an accolade from Ben: 'Will I do a concert here next year for the new concert hall and the 20th festival?' 'Yes of course Ben,' I say. At once, sitting in the parish church hearing but I fear not listening to, lovely early Byrd, I started panicking about new material for the event.

12 June 1966

Pretty pearly morning after a wet night. We *may* play some tennis – Reggie has gone to book courts.

Am much amused by the funny little behaviourisms of the Big Guns here. They are at a disadvantage in being so recognisable, so evidently the reason and the centre of it all, and they have cultivated ways of seeing and not getting involved. During a boring endless slow Danish encore sung by the little sailor-suited Boys Choir I amused myself by writing a jingle on this subject:

> Ben smiles,
> Peter smiles,
> But Imogen lowers her head
> And scurries.
> The festival weighs a ton on her,
> I mustn't add to her worries.

> Ben smiles,
> Peter smiles,
> But Imo avoids recognising
> Saving herself – for what? one wonders.
> Her modesty *is* surprising.

Absolutely unpolished and bitchy. And *private*. It is funny to see her *not* seeing me!

13 June 1966

Before the concert we went for drinks with Ingaret and Laurens van der Post to meet J.B. Priestley and his Jacquetta Hawkes. Priestley is not attractive – he is anti so much and unappetising, there's a stultifying narrowness of being anti, mind closed.

Jacquetta Hawkes is very anti too. She has very narrow lips and doesn't look one in the eye. Clever yes, shy perhaps. But not cosy, and we sensed a strain. J.B. paints rather well – took it up ten years ago, he showed us a perceptive sketch he did in forty minutes that morning.

14 June 1966
In the afternoon we attended Julian Bream and his pupil partner John Williams in guitars for two. With Peter P. doing some very spikey setting of lovely Yeats poems by one Warren, born 1928. I didn't find these in any way pleasing except for P.P.'s beautiful singing of the ungrateful notes.

After lunch we went to Snape to look at the Maltings and discover which bits of it is to be the new concert hall. The roof is off and it looks ready to start, big and very well placed. One end will be a restaurant. Reggie went to look for his kingfisher down the estuary while I heard Heather Harper sing Britten's *Les Illuminations* most beautifully. It's poems of Arthur Rimbaud you know.

16 June 1966
We had endless rain today and were rather cross about it after the flawless days on end this summer.

In the evening it was *Acis and Galatea* with lovely handle music and excellent singing. Eliz. Harewood has a lovely voice: a real pleasure giver. It is set in a Watteau picture, with matching costumes, stylised gestures and a lot of stillness. But I don't think Handel *can* be staged. How ignorant one is: suddenly the one-eyed Polyphemus, bass, opened up to sing what one imagines is to be a villain's song and what does it turn out to be? 'O ruddier than the cherry'! Surprise surprise!

Now we are off to the parish church for the memorial to Edith Sitwell. Wonder how it will be.

This morning Reggie went off to bird while I went to hear Imogen Holst give a lecture on 'What is Musical History?'

Dull you might think? It was utterly fascinating and absolutely first class. She came on trippingly, head down. Not a trace of powder or lipstick on that 15th century head painted on wood. A pale beige dress blending in with face and hair. Almost invisible really. It was a miracle of erudition, simplicity, interest, passion and <u>wit</u>.

She took us back to the first known music in which two parts were used. After centuries of plainsong the 11th century monks in Spain embroidered a line of sound in and out, over and under the plainsong. While the Purcell Singers demonstrated, she asked us to imagine hearing this for the first time. I was well away in a bare stone monastery, and I heard it new!

Then a piece of Bach cantata that Mozart heard being rehearsed in Leipzig cathedral. His first hearing of Bach and he was bowled over. Imo read us a contemporary eye-witness report: after the rehearsals he got hold of the parts and spread them on the floor, on chairs and his knees and exclaimed with joy at what he saw. Later in *The Magic Flute* he quotes the actual cantata.

Then she told us how, when Ben was nine years old and at prep school, thus we can date this revelation, he went to a music shop in Lowestoft, and he found an early two-part song for women's voices by Gustav Holst. It was his very first contact with modern music.

Imogen was caustic about critics who write of 'tendencies' who say that a composer is 'paving a way'. 'What they are doing' she said 'is making music, not "creating tendencies".'

At the end she made us all sing a ten-part round, and that was a triumph for we did – first time.

19 June 1966

Last night we had some wonderful Purcell. Best of all Janet Baker and April Cantello doing a minor lament for Queen Mary of such ravishment that I wanted it all over again at once. Janet Baker is the most popular singer there is now, they stamped and yelled for her and I agreed.

After dinner the rockets went up and all Aldeburgh came running along the front to see the lifeboat launched. Such a pretty sight. It rescued a yacht and towed it to Harwich. Quite a night for the lifeboat boys.

The late night concerts are my favourite really. I love the quiet walk up the hill to the huge East Anglian church, the silence, the lack of applause and the music done superbly, and then quietly back here again. Reggie is usually asleep by then.

The Festival Party in the Jubilee Hall was really great fun. Excellent food and wine is a gift from a huge fat Herr von Schubert.

Julian Bream played some jazzed up Bach – superb. Surprise item Peter Pears singing 'The owl and the pussy cat' in an amusing setting. Then a jam session with Emanuel Hurwitz (first fiddle of orchestra), Julian B. and a double bass, and, unrehearsed, Peter, doing 'Night and day'. His rhythm was appalling! No feel for the beat at all. Wasn't it interesting. A gay evening.

Aldeburgh has been *such* fun. Best year so far for weather and birds and music.

London
20 June 1966

My Dear Ben

Very reluctantly we left Aldeburgh today after yet another wonderful festival. Either they get better year by year or else it is that one's perception and appreciation deepens – anyway this was a *beauty* and I write to thank you very much for doing so much for us all.

The something 'special' about this festival stems from the qualities you and Peter bring to it and I think this touches some responsive spring in all of those who come in touch with it, that is why it is so richly satisfying and so entirely different form anywhere else in the world where they have festivals.

June is a magic month in Suffolk and the drive over to Orford for *Fiery Furnace*, in a faint summer haze with long blue shadows was breathtaking. Long blue shadows and the wind had dropped. Ditches full of Queen Anne's lace, wild roses, elderflower in full cream, and a nightingale sang in the churchyard, as we were going in! Such production!

love Joyce G.

1967

After 20 years of concerts held in village halls and local churches, Britten's dream was fulfilled in 1967 when a derelict agricultural building, a few miles inland from Aldeburgh at Snape, was converted into the Maltings concert hall with 750 seats.

The 1967 programme began with the official opening by the Queen and ended three weeks later with Purcell's The Fairy Queen. *Other events included Angus Wilson lecturing on the* Red Herring; *a new production of Britten's* A Midsummer Night's Dream; *William Plomer reading poetry; Julian Bream playing guitar and a talk on Anglo-Saxon Ship-Burials.*

Britten had also invited Joyce to perform and although she felt 'it is a challenge to keep up to the standard you and Peter give!', she accepted. Joyce was an unusual, though very popular, choice for the programme: she was well aware that her sell-out shows subsidised the more esoteric concerts.

London
30 May 1967

My dear Ben

We're looking forward to coming back to Aldeburgh like *anything*.

I wonder if you could spare 10 or 15 minutes at some point perhaps on Monday morning? I'd be grateful if you'd hear a little item I've written as a surprise for the Festival. But I think surprises can be a shock and therefore if you didn't like the idea of it being done in the programme I won't. In case this make you feel very uneasy I hasten to say it's a piece in praise. There is a little sun out here for the moment.

Love Joyce

Wentworth Hotel, Aldeburgh, Suffolk
1 June 1967

Darling Ginnie,

The Grenfells' Luggage! How I wish I knew how to travel light! I have just counted THIRTEEN pieces AND stage dresses AND four coats.

We came in via Snape and went to see the new Hall. It's so attractive. The walls inside are red brick and the wood appears to be blonde and unstained. The chairs are the same, with cane seats and backs. All so light and rural looking, without being in the least 'folksy'. *Very* spacious and gay looking. Designed by the Danish Ove Arup.

We found John Piper putting the finishing touches to some large posterish coloured panels in the foyer. All a bit garish. The place was stiff with people doing last minute jobs. Drink was being delivered to the fascinating restaurant with big windows looking straight out over the marsh. The BBC were everywhere. So were the film boys who are making the documentary I'm to be in on Thursday. We had a good look round while it was comparatively empty, for tomorrow's crowds won't allow much exploring and HMQ will be in all the best places. I'd say it's a great success as a building – lots of parking space, a big lawn with a huge Henry Moore on it looks well, and the theatre skilfully built within the walls of the original Maltings.

4 June 1967

Today the sun oozed in and out of haze. R went off birding and I bought a little red sailing-cap with a bobble on top to wear for 'Ethel' – the girl who goes mad at football games. I've revived it and it's really far more apt in 1967 than it was in 1954. Thank heaven.

After dinner the two one-act operas, first performances, by Lennox Berkeley and William Walton. My view is that neither really works. Walton's is bravura old hat and *far* too long. *The Bear* by Chekhov rewritten to be sung by Paul Dehn. *The Castaway*, out of Homer, is static and rather dry but I liked it far more because it was tighter and clearer. Neither is first-class and all the lavish lighting, décor and excellent singing *can't* disguise this – ever.

The Grenfells often joined the Red House tennis parties with Ben Britten, Peter Pears and the van der Posts. Joyce and Reggie first met playing tennis but it was not until middle-age that they found their accuracy and energy had actually improved and it became a central part of their relaxation.

Bang-bang in Israel. Oh Lor … surely we won't have to go and meddle, will we?

R. and I played tennis with Laurens and Ingaret van der Post until poor Ingaret fell backwards and did herself an injury to her wrist. They are so strong at tennis. Laurens is very agile and accurate and moves like a boy. She, too, is unmarked by time, with a girl's figure and vigour. Astonishing vitality and zest. Like teenagers: boney, quick, accurate and *strong*! I was amazed.

R. and I plodded rather but were fairly accurate if dull. I mind not making contact, because it is so boring, but I don't care a jot – or a tittle – who *wins* so long as I am in the game, under some sort of control. Don't mind being out-played a bit. Do mind missing shots, mis-timing and failing to *look at the ball*.

My show is tonight and this morning Bill and I went up to the Red House to sing our Bené song to the Master himself. Bill spent all yesterday afternoon writing out his jazz accompaniment so he gets it right! I have never toiled, polished, worked on anything as I have on this ditty. I was praying that he would like it.

As we arrived the beautiful new Steinway was being returned to Ben's library cum music room after being used at Blythburgh church, so we sat in the garden in hot sun with cool glasses in our hands talking Festival.

Then into the long room full of good modern pictures and soft light coming in from all sides. I sang it well and the reaction was *so* extraordinary that I was quite flummoxed. Ben ran to me and embraced me, weeping! He was *very* touched and moved. It was very dear and *entirely* unexpected. Clearly it *had* moved him. Peter too. So we were rewarded.

Permission granted, Joan and Bill Blezard lunched and we had a tremendous discussion about treating creative artists. I said we *all* have a need for kid-gloves – certainly in the early stages of work. Encouragement is vital at that stage and must come before criticism. Joan agrees with Viola that the *objective* is the point – the music in their instance – and this must always come first and, roughly, to hell with feelings of artists. But I know that unless the artistic creature is reassured (or this artistic creature, anyhow!) in the very early stages, the objective isn't reached.

Then Bill and I met at the theatre and worked. Under difficulties. The piano had no pedals! It had been moved in but not totally reassembled and the man responsible was not to be found. However dear Bert Pearce, Steinway's genius and charmer, came to tune it and got it together for us. There was a lot of dust about because curtains were used that hadn't been used before and whoosh there were moats and beams everywhere.

The programme went well and our song was rapturously received. I was dying to sing it again but didn't feel there had been quite enough *specific* call for that! Later everyone said 'Why didn't you sing it again?' Damn. Lost me only chance. For it's a one-occasion song.

The song was a 'recitative' set to swing music by Blezard, full of puns on 'Ben' – benefactor, bene, beneficial, benign. The middle verse went:

How *ben*evolent is the setting
Suffolk winds *ben*ignly blow
*Ben*efitting all who came here
And to concerts go oh-oh-oh
Seats *ben*umb on Parish church *ben*ches

But the *ben*efited ear recognises *ben*ediction
In the wonders it can hear
*Ben*e, *ben*e molto *ben*e.

Joyce also performed her monologue 'Artist's room', in which music fans go backstage to see the pianist after a recital. A top-price ticket holder says: 'Beethoven does go on, doesn't he, bless his heart. Just when you think he's finished, the entire thing starts again.'

Joyce added a new character, Marty Winderhaur, an American student. She is writing a thesis on the sonata form and gives the concert pianist some advice:

'I quite liked the way you expose the contours of the sonata. ...Although it conflicts with interpretations I have familiarised myself with on disc. Still ... I think it is valid, but I would very much like to discuss with you the premises from which you tangentised your explorations. I think I could say I derived some intellectual satisfaction from your performance, but, urm, my emotions were only semi-engaged by your display of pyrotechnics. But I thought it was cogent. Yehs, it was quite cogent.'

7 June 1967

Over to Westleton for lunch with Ben and Peter in the Crown pub. Such delicious food! Rare roast beef wrapped in light pastry and green salad. Ben was fascinating talking about music – about the approach to new works: painting too. He isn't a Beethoven man but conceded his greatness though says he doesn't like the way Beethoven shouts so much.

8 June 1967

At Minsmere we heard the bittern boom and then saw it clearly for quite some time. The real thrill was very rare: the male marsh harrier (only three or four pairs in the whole of GB) flew across the marsh with its claws full of prey. Could have been a baby rabbit or a rat. The female flew up to meet him and he dropped the prey and she caught it in mid air! Sensational. The Prince of Hesse was in raptures.

Last night it was the new production of *A Midsummer Night's Dream* at the Maltings. It's very good, looks pretty and was beautifully directed by Colin Graham. Viola is the repetiteur and was at the harpsichord and celeste in the pit, looking very pretty in a black chiffon-topped jacket. Have hardly seen her! She's been rehearsing all day and night.

9 June 1967

Ice cold here – I was back into a thick-er vest in a trice for warm*pth*. Met R. at Jubilee Hall to hear William Plomer read his poems and Julian Bream to play his guitar. Lobos and Grieg and a modern Martin. It was easy on the ear. Plomer is a good poet. You can understand what he is about and his use of words and images flared in my mind, so I had a lovely time. I like his light stuff much less: but there is a new unpublished straight one about the exuberance in Bavarian church decoration that I love.

I can't read about Egypt and Israel, can you? Too much of it.

13 June 1967

I painted three (or four) pictures yesterday. I tried to paint washing in a line, it billowed and waved and was *impossible* but so lovely in the brilliant light. No good but I begin to see how one reduces the detail to the essence, it really is what one leaves out that seems to make the mark. Strange. Like *everything*, it takes time and practice.

R. is asleep and about to snore. I will whistle as that usually works. Love to you.

Viola came to lunch looking very gay in a bright magenta linen coat, the same shape as Nehru used to wear. She had a mossy green skirt below it and magenta shoes.

On Friday she was given 24 hours to learn Ben's fantastically tricky First Piano Concerto, in order to rehearse it with Richter most of Saturday! (She had to play the whole orchestral part.) She's a brilliant sight-reader and rose to the challenge of this complex and exuberant concerto. Richter was very nervous of this work – it is fiendishly difficult and full of notes, but he played it superbly with the New Philharmonia Orchestra under Ben yesterday.

This was the first time I'd heard a full orchestra in the Maltings. It was so marvellous to be able to hear all the parts so clearly even in the full out FFF passages. The First Concerto was written when Ben was twenty-seven and is complex and exuberant and altogether entertaining. We raised the roof in appreciation. For me the high spot was Ben's conducting of the overture of *The Magic Flute*. It was so fresh and beautiful!

We drove back afterwards still vibrating with music and sun and pleasure. In the evening, a perfect contrast, a miniature recital of madrigals sung round a table by Peter Pears and a consort of perfectly balanced voices – Lully, Campion, Dowland and some lute songs. The whole thing lit and poised and beautifully realised by Peter.

Once again, Joyce wrote to Britten:

21 June 1967

My dear Ben

Every year I think: this was the best festival of all. This year I know it was! There seems to be a new spaciousness and growth about it that has come with the beautiful hall at Snape.

There is something about the Aldeburgh Festival that makes you want to do far better than you have ever done before anywhere else in the world. Funnily enough it isn't just egotism. It is a challenge to keep up to the standard you and Peter both give – which goes far beyond the line of duty!

One wants to do one's own job just that much more freely, just that much more clearly and deeply. And better!

It's a little frightening but it's very exciting and I am very grateful to have the chance to play here. So I thank you very much for having us, Bill Blezard and me.

When I was in London last week I made a little disc of the 20th festival song he and I wrote for you and Peter and here it is as a small memento, to say thank you and to commemorate the 1967 Festival. It comes with love. No good trying to pick out favourite things from the programme but the G minor Mozart – and your piano concerto – these are special alright.

With love from Joyce

Joyce left this letter and record in the front hall of the Red House. Three years later Britten found it, unopened, at the back of a cupboard.

The Red House, Aldeburgh

Dear Joyce

I do hope this letter reaches you in a forgiving mood! Peter and I were hunting for an ancient record in a seldom used cupboard, and to our great surprise, then delight, and then horror, we found a record you'd sent us, away back in 1967, which neither of us had seen before. I can only imagine it was 'tidied away', imagining that we had seen it. I do hope that you will forgive my not having thanked for the precious copy of your handsome and delightful Tribute. I somehow think you will forgive, for you are so grand a person.

Joyce replied:

Of course I understand and of course I forgive! What's more I can imagine the wave of horror you felt when you discovered the record and you have my deepest sympathy.

After this, the record was put away among Britten's papers and forgotten. It was only rediscovered in 2005, mislabelled but still in perfect condition.

1968

Wentworth, Aldeburgh, Suffolk
8 June 1968

Darling Virginia

It's a *stinker* here. Grey sea – grey sky – grey rain. However we have our pleasant room and good beds and lots of constant Hot, so we are not complaining but are grateful (for a *great* many other things too!) All is very lush here now. Hedges are thick and the Queen Anne's lace is frothing in ditches for miles on end. We saw our first wild rose and the elder flowers are starting to turn from green to cream. It's mighty pretty. I love the eighteenth century wooden houses and the untouched feeling of the country here. Cottages have new pink wash.

I like finding this place the same only a bit better each time. We have a new blue carpet and a new blue armchair cover. But Edna still smiles when she brings in the breakfast tray, the odd-man still grunts as he lugs cases up to the second floor, and John the head waiter is welcoming as ever. And the flowers are beautiful in the hall, and many of the same people are here for the festival and not looking any older.

We came via Snape, where the Henry Moore has been changed. That was a two-piece job, faintly human. Now there seem to be two largish rounds of stone with holes, matching, and painted pale turquoise blue. The holes I mean. It doesn't look like a Moore. Must be a Barbara Hepworth.

The oil on the beaches has been cleared at last – it's over a year since Torrey Canyon sank. Reggie had crab for dinner and said it was scrummy.

9 June 1968

I went to Lettice Coleman's house for a pre-lunch drink to see Luciana Arrighi. The house was full of young men in partly fancy dress. One had a polo necked shirt made of pink gingham. Another had exaggerated bell-bottom trousers. There was long hair. All were very pleasant and friendly, and Luci looked entrancing in a skin-tight black silk polo-necked sweater and very tight black Levis. Low on her hips was a Victorian gilt chatelaine!

After P. Pears sang like a bird in *The Seasons* at Snape, we found John Gielgud all alone so we said do join us for dinner if you have nothing better to do. He was in good form and full of funny theatre anecdotes. Rather a bitchy story about Emlyn Williams going backstage to see Gladys Cooper somewhere on tour, quite lately. He passed two very elderly ladies at the stage door, and one said to the other, 'I wish I hadn't let you see her, she *used* to be so graceful.'

Another about Noël telephoning across the Atlantic to sympathise with Clifton Webb over the death of his million-years-old mother. Clifton Webb was famous for being very stingy. He was crying down the telephone to Noël and Noël said, 'Clifton, if you don't stop crying I shall reverse the charges'!

10 June 1968

John's Shakespeare recital, in the Jubilee Hall, was a huge success and a most remarkable performance, he has such a range and the voice seems more beautiful than ever. Sitting behind us was a middle-aged fan who suddenly said to the man next to her, a total stranger, 'Why don't you applaud? Aren't you enjoying it?' He said he was, but felt the relationship between artist and audience to be personal, and that was his way. She was not to be put off, and insisted he applaud, with a missionary zeal!

Only three people went backstage to see John so we hovered and walked him back to the hotel under a full moon making a wide dazzle path down the sea. Then sat up until midnight talking while he unwound.

11 June 1968

Well, our hectic life of Pleasure and the Arts, mingled with Sport continues.

This afternoon Janet Baker singing most beautifully two unknown (to me) Purcell songs of enormous wonder, then a modern song cycle *The Wife of Winter* by David Lord, who was born 1944 and came on at the end in a tousle of hair and wool and looked like a toy teddy of about twelve years old. She sang it very well, but I am bored by these scatterings – all on the themes of horror and unhappiness. She ended on Warlock which was lovely. A relief! (I'm like all the old ladies who sigh with pleasure when the music is pleasing!)

We were bowled over by Britten's new opera *The Prodigal Son* and Orford and the dusk and the setting. It was a heavenly occasion. A pretty dove-coloured evening twilight. Soft and subtle. The air tense with the excitement that Ben's new works always bring with them.

All the regulars were there in force and we had wonderful seats. When it was over there was a *long* sustained and powerful silence. It's a lovely piece. John Shirley-Quirk sang the father supremely well. Young Robert Tear played the younger son most movingly. Peter Pears was the Tempter–narrator and looked rather awful in a high black (net and wire?) hat as if made of petals in flame shapes. He had an eye mask and a blonde wig and beard and was not exactly tempting! But very evil. Alas, I detected rather a sign or two of wear in that remarkable voice, and after hearing the young ones in such form it showed rather. *Sad.* But he was, as always such a real craftsman that one was full of admiration. It is full of invention and movement. We loved it. Many are saying it's *the* best. I still love *Fiery Furnace*, but this is a very close second.

Andrew Porter of the *Financial Times* loved *The Prodigal Son* and has written most illuminatingly about it. I'm always fascinated to see what I missed at the time – such as the great significance of key signatures and the subtlety of using a horn here or a viola there… ! Only the cognoscenti really ever get the full flavour of anything I fear. As a laywoman I had a very good time in Orford Church, now I want to hear it all again in the light of further information.

E.M. Forster and William Plomer lunched next to us. We walked down the High Street with Desmond Shawe-Taylor. The places hisses with the sibilance of highly intellectual non-marryers. They seem to swarm here, all shapes, sizes and ages.

While I was listening desperately to the advanced horror music this morning – a dire piece of deadly pounding in earnest on the piano – I made myself laugh with an obituary I thought all too possible:

'She died from opening her mind too far.'

13 June 1968

Today pale and gusty, dry is the *mot juste*. I got full of grit yesterday out on the marsh. I put my hair in rollers under my yachting/cricketing/fishing hat and looked very bizarre, but they are used to eccentrics in these parts. Bert conducted us to Minsmere where we saw a splendid spoonbill. We had a lovely view of all sorts of visiting birds as well as natives. One hide is in trees on the edge of the wood and the marsh, sheltered and quiet, bliss. I was so glad to be in it all among little singing birds, wrens, nightingales, etc and could have happily stayed *there* all day.

Lady Dashwood seems easier this year. Either R. and I are mellowing and more loving, or people *are* all much nicer. Both no doubt!

Having hair washed at 'Cordelia' *coiffeest* in the High later, love Joyce.

16 June 1968

Last night there was a party sitting at the next table to us that defied belief. Alfred and Clementine Beit, and Vivien Mosley, who was my bridesmaid 40 years ago. She looks intelligent and nice; large, busty and handsome, with a low voice that carries, but it was Clementine's that rang out and shamed me! There was lot of loud chat about music, and it was so funny and *so* insensitive to give free opinions FFF in the dining room of the Wentworth in Festival Time! Ears were on stalks all round, and when Alfred said Britten can't write a tune I thought perhaps a thunderbolt might hit him! The Australian painter Sidney Nolan and wife were at the table the other side of the group and could hardly eat for listening. They discussed modern art and I dreaded they might talk about Sidney, but they simply dismissed the later Picassos, acclaimed Rembrandt, and then took to discussing their friends.

They were really rather terrible and once again I felt ashamed of my class and disassociated myself from it! It is the total disregard of other people that is so unattractive. And so arrogant. I think, possibly, this group was quite intelligent and not at all nasty, but they exposed their folly so lavishly that even John, the head waiter, gave me a loud understanding wink as he passed us! I do think it's time there was a social change, roll on the tumbrels.

If *I* was nice, I wouldn't even have written to you about it!

17 June 1968

Viola came to lunch in good heart and a pink tweed jacket and skirt. She had to go off to Orford afterwards to rehearse a second cast in *Prodigal* for tonight, but managed to get to the Maltings for the second half of the Tchaikovsky concert. This morning she plays modern Samuel Barber songs sung by Heather Harper at the dear Jubilee Hall. You see the sort of hours the musicians have to work!

18 June 1968

There is a thick white fog. The sea is very still and the sound of little waves turning on the shingle is very quiet after some of the poundings we've had. It's like November.

On goes the Festival and it gets better and better. Yesterday morning Viola played for Heather Harper singing a cycle of songs by Samuel Barber to texts from early Irish poems translated from Gaelic. They were lovely and both Heather and Viola were on top form. It was an all modern programme and the Jubilee Hall wasn't quite full. Sad because it was a very enjoyable and not at all frightening concert! Only a harp solo by Ossian Ellis was a bore. *He* is *never* a bore, but the piece he had to play was. My heart sinks when a piece of music starts slowly with single notes widely spaced and apparently quite without relationship. It was one of those.

Then dear Mstislav Rostropovich and his cello, unaccompanied in the perfection of acoustics of that lovely Maltings. I do not much like unaccompanied *anything* (except voice) *unless* it is Mstislav or Casals. Then I can sit back and know all is well. First Bach in C major and the whole thing was just exactly right. It looked so marvellous too, small stocky Russian married to golden brown cello set against very high curving screens in pale grey straw colour on pale wood floor, and the vaulted ceiling of the great hall, unstained wood again, rising way up above it all. Light was good, and concentrated only on the figure on its tiny platform. I pined to draw it and even measured out with my mind's eye that the height of the hall was seven times the height of Rostropovich and cello.

After Bach, Ben's First Cello Sonata, originally played for the first performance by Rostropovich about three years ago. After the interval came the first performance of his Second Cello Sonata and this one is even lovelier. Much easier to assimilate on first hearing, very melodic and lyrical. Great enthusiasm for it and for the Russian and for Ben. Lots of hugging, kissing, the Russo manner and a lot of playful pushing each other forward all of which delighted the house, and rather embarrassed Ben.

I've seen lots of familiar faces, and *so* many I know for smiling at but haven't a notion of their names.

The setting was seen at its most lovely at six yesterday, the marsh was blonde and bland under a cloudless sky. Not a breath of wind. I do think the Maltings is the most pleasing – certainly the most beautifully set – concert hall in the world.

20 June 1968

Very promising haze. Windless. Fog horns in distance.

Yesterday we were quite drunk with fresh air and birds. In particular a very pleasing lapwing with two babies which she tucked under her, and they all sat cosily on a duckboard. Many bearded tits and two bittern. No booms though.

Back for a cupper in time for Rostropovich playing two cello concerti by Shostakovich at the Maltings. Norman del Mar conducted a *much* augmented English Chamber Orchestra. These are very noisy pieces with a great deal of activity going on in the kitchen department. He uses three drums, bells, wooden slates, whips, and various other devices making sounds of steam, gravel. One is never bored. Too much goes on at a great pace and with a lot of noise. The cello goes through every possible hoop and Rostropovich played it superbly. So we were all excited but I *didn't* like it although I admired the energy. But musically? It was like a 1930s factory impression. Lots of big gun sounds – James Blades pounded away with very satisfying thwacks.

Afterwards dinner with Laurens and Ingaret van der Post and we discussed the student revolt in Paris. They want to abolish all exams. Wonder if our lot *will* abolish the House of Lords? In many ways it is rather anachronistic. It is archaic to be ruled by those whose only qualifications is the accident of birth. At least, *most* of them have inherited titles. I suppose if it was all appointed it might be a useful extra House?

The sun is now making pale sequin sparks on a lazy sea.

Last night's performance of *The Prodigal Son* was even more moving. It's a *marvellous* piece of work and I am so glad we were able to see it again. It was a pretty rather then dramatic evening. Huge navy blue clouds with pale green patches of calm in between, and now all the elder flowers and wild roses are out, so the journey to Orford was a constant blessing on the eye. I do love Suffolk. (Cumberland is for special. Suffolk is a possible for living in I think.) We sat at the back of the church this time on a raised platform and from there we had a far batter idea of the production as a *whole* and it is masterly. Colin Graham is a genius for this sort of thing. It's a perfect work of art.

Reggie thought so too. His *real* enjoyment of the concerts and events here is one of the most lovely bonuses to have. He gets enormous delight from *watching* even when he isn't interested in the sounds.

24 June 1968

My dear Ben

Toynbee said something to the effect that civilization isn't a harbour it's a journey, and I'm very grateful to you for being one of the present day pilots. It has been the BEST of festivals, in depth as well as in height and breadth.

Love Joyce. Reggie send his gratitude too.

1969

Among Joyce's friends in Aldeburgh was the painter Mary 'Att' Potter, who lived in a bungalow-cum-studio in the garden of the Red House. Joyce first met her in 1939 when she was married to Stephen Potter, radio producer and author of Gamesmanship. *Over the years, the Grenfells bought several of Mary's paintings and in 1969 she painted Joyce's portrait. Mary was clear about her working conditions – no music, no talk and sitting only in the morning.*

Red Studio, Aldeburgh, Suffolk
3 February 1969

Darling Virginia,

Deep snow here and it's pretty as can be and oh-so inconvenient. My car is shrouded and soon I will arise and put on my snow-boots. Att has made it pretty with many ancient pieces but modern linen curtains and as well as her own pictures there are pretty 18th century prints and a jugful of winter shrubs in bloom. And a log fire. A friendly gay house.

She wanted to see what I had brought to wear for the picture. She's a girl for pastel colours so I'll put on a spencer under that flimsy white nylon and I may even squeeze a sweater under too unless I look too bulbous. She is very particularly about the light and can't paint unless it is exactly as she wants it.

I refilled my pen with utmost care but there has been a mysterious tiny splatter on the *sheet*. Ghastly social bloomer.

4 February 1969

Att has made a very good start – all the most delectable colour – pale turquoise background, white blouse, pinky face and grey-blue eyes. She paints with implications and indications rather than absolutely photographic detail. The slightest unfinished look is deliberate and very successful. She is most dedicated and is, literally, absent while she works. Little grunts and moans but no conversation and her concentration is absolute. This is very restful and I sit there doing my own thoughts and wafting away.

24 February 1969

Last night Ben B. dined. He is so strange. One gets *fairly* near but as with all people of genius there are whole areas of total privacy. He is also fairly confident in B.B. in *some* ways and *not* in others. He is very concerned at the number of appeals for musical help from young composers; from teachers about young pupils; from mothers about young talented offspring. The demands for time are increasing and persistent – time to look at scores, hear performances, see and talk to budding artist/composers, etc. If he gave up composing and conducting he might be able to cope but as it is, the things pile up; scores arrive and sit unopened, etc.

It really is a problem and I suppose a common one for anyone of his stature and known interest in young people. He is, as he says, pleased to be asked. But how important is it that he should use up very precious time for this in preference to his work? But he had a lot of help when he was young and I think he feels bound to do the same for other people. There is a faintly – and I meant faint – malicious streak that is apparently latent in a lot of these rather feminine men. I think that he could be ruthless, merciless? It is part of the insecurity of such a position, no doubt. He is very agreeable to meet; generous about talent in others – he spoke enthusiastically of Heather Harper, of Viola and all her work.

This afternoon Peter P. was out exercising his miniature

dachshund. He looked marvellously handsome with his white hair blowing and his good bones and that attractive smile. He had on a long scarf like an undergrad, and there is a sort of eternal undergrad something about him, isn't there? I think it is because he has, with all his enormous scholarship and maturity, kept his first enthusiasm. That's one of the most attractive qualities anyone can have, don't you agree?

Wentworth Hotel, Aldeburgh, Suffolk
Saturday 7 June 1969

Lovely to be here again. We both start beaming as we get into East Anglia and particularly in June for the Festival. England at its perfect best; those little villages with pink and pale yellow washed houses standing in gardens with peonies bursting into ruby red and pink and white, and wisteria and laburnum drips. Chestnut trees can never have had a heavier weight of candles. And not a cloud in the sky.

It's the second day of the festival and a feast of Purcell, Mozart and Schubert with the Amadeus Quartet. What a dream of a hall the Maltings is. The *Trout* Quintet as a finale with Ben at the piano. It was *magical*. The whole thing rose and flew – or maybe swam is a better verb. Anyway a lovely treat.

We came back through green hedges and dog daisies and wild roses, with a wind like a knife stirring them all into frantic bobbing and bending. Earlier it was a dazzling day with cerulean blue skies and everything glistened and glowed. I tried to paint some washing on a line – it billowed and waved and was *impossible* but so lively in the brilliant light.

R. has gone to collect Bill, who was playing for a TV 'Play School' all day. Now we will be complete until Joan has to whip up to London on Monday to give a lecture at her musical college, but gets down in time for the evening concert.

Many old faces, all looking splendid, which is comforting. Lady Dashwood in purple, still moo-erning the late lamented Sir John, do you suppose? Or maybe she is also a *mauvais sujet* like Lady Willingdon? The Miller Joneses, the Princess of Hesse with a huge Hohenloe niece who looks rather cross and Germanic.

Sunday 8 June 1969

We heard the news of the fire at 8 a.m. on our radio and can hardly believe it. There it was yesterday, so beautiful, so airy, so absolutely the dream of what a concert hall in a country place should be.

Now … all gone. The mind boggles at the mammoth task of coping with all of us and our tickets for concerts at the Maltings. Reggie has gone down to offer our help in any clerical or practical way as needed. Someone will have to cope with the crowds and the reorganising. Ben was up all night of course. Peter, too, no doubt.

Most of the concerts, and all of the big drawing-power events, were to have been at the Maltings. Orford and Blythburgh are to be used we heard but they don't hold the numbers. I think there will have to be parallel concerts to absorb us all – while some go to Orford others will be in the Jubilee? Or that awful WI hut place in Thorpeness? It's a task alright.

We were to have gone to the Maltings for a huge choral concert with Ben and Peter tonight. … I'll telephone later.

Monday 9 June 1969

The shock of the fire was considerable. R. and I couldn't believe it. We, too, saw the news on ITV Anglia last night and it was a horrid sight. That beautiful biscuit-coloured auditorium with its beautiful old brick walls and perfect acoustics had become something very special already. One felt real affection for it as we went into it on Saturday afternoon. It was looking its best, too, all scrubbed and clean and palely Scandinavian. Outside the marsh simmered in dazzling light and stirred under the damnable wind, which apparently whipped up the fire.

One was pleased to see the familiar faces, some plumper, some greyer, some in the same clothes as 1968, some in patently new wear.

Yesterday morning we played tennis *à trois* – R., Bill and me, while Joan corrected students' papers and marked the score of a Mozart piece she is to conduct this week. Bill worked out a complex system so that each of us, when serving alone, had one service with the sun behind him. He made out we'd played sixty games in all! But R. says it was more like thirty-five. Even so …

After lunch we drove to a field full of hay bales and settled by a fallen-down straw rick out of the wind, and *boiling*. R. and B. read the papers and zizzed. Joan corrected and marked up and I did sketches of the recumbent fellers sprawled in the tumbled straw. Accompanied by Radio 3, but after a time harpsichord alone seemed less desirable than silence and larks, so we switched off. A *little* harpsichord goes a long way. … Did you know it has been likened to two skeletons copulating on a tin roof? Vivid but less accurate, I think, than Sheila Lynd's immortal 'playing on a bird cage with a toasting fork'.

I don't think Lady Dashwood is in mourning, for last night she was in white with a vibrant magenta shawl like a Casa Pupo rug.

Tell you wot: I wish you were here. Love. Love.

11 June 1969

Today to Blythburgh, where a real job has been done in two days to turn it into a concert hall. Amazing. Carpenters and elecs.

have worked *all* night; wardrobe, too, I believe, and we were given an impeccable performance of *Idomeneo*. It is full of such *beautiful* music and of course Ben got every nuance out of it. I found the whole occasion such a triumph of *spirit*. Very moving to know how hard people will work when they feel it is *needed*. A great tribute to Ben and all who have made the Festival such an *actual* thing. Marvellous. I couldn't see Viola and her harpsichord but acoustics are lovely in Blythburgh and I heard her beautifully. Heather Harper sang like an angel.

12 June 1969

Yesterday we both helped in the Festival Office for a couple of hours in the morning, addressing envelopes for receipts of money sent in for the Maltings fund. They have had a wonderful response and such dear letters. One woman, either elderly or ill or both, or poor? wrote to say she had never been to Aldeburgh or the Festival and didn't suppose she ever would but that she was so grateful for Ben's music and Peter's singing that she was enclosing £3. The local Borough Council, who are a bit jealous of the Maltings and haven't been very co-operative, have relented and sent £1,000 interest-free loan. There is a lot of Love generating around the whole place.

13 June 1969

This sea is shimmering silky and the fisherman's flag on the hut opposite this window is hanging almost motionless. It's been whipped to a frenzy until today.

Lady Dashwood wears little girl shifts in bright colours, so her mourning is definitely over.

Viola is Continuo in *Idomeneo*; in *Prodigal Son* as assistant to Ben; in two or three concerts as duet partner with Ben; and as accompanist to Peter P. So she's got a very full plate. She looks better but still walks badly although she says her leg starts to *feel* better.

We drove home in an exquisite *crépuscule*. A rosy sunset, deep masses of cow parsley and white may trees. It is being a lovely time. All love, darling.

16 June 1969

This morning is all mist and distant foghorns. I got up at 7 to do my hair and face, and there was a man sitting on a little stool on the beach painting what can only be a very Whistlerish blur.

We went over to Blythburgh church sitting in its hayfield of a cemetery and in it we heard a thrilling performance of the Intro and Allegro for Strings of Elgar. Ben conducted. It made me cry! Then Imo in a black long shift and jacket conducted her father's charming and gay suite that has the folksong 'If all the world was paper' in it. And then a tremendously cheerful Mass in B by Haydn sung for all its considerable worth by Heather Harper, Janet Baker and two unknown gents and the Aldeburgh Festival Choir. It was a real rouser. Talk about Joyful Noises unto the Lord!

18 June 1969

Rains are lashing but even so I watched a stout party, female, in a sky-blue bathing-suit go for a long bathe. Glutton for punishment.

Last night to Ben and Peter's Red House for a drinks party to meet *eighty* Hesse students in the big music room. It is always an Occasion and the young are thrilled to be so near the great men. They are a fairly ordinary looking lot this year. Sideboards, some ringlets, gold-rimmed glasses, and enviable heads of silky blonde fairness.

Reggie and I did a mooch in which I bought him a very gay

mustard tweed jacket to replace his old much loved greeny grey that has actually fallen apart, and I can't go on rebuilding it any longer.

For no reason I simply could not get to sleep. The last time I looked it was 3 a.m. My lover and friend lay on his back and made the most maddening little snores that rose to a climax, resulting in a snort, and then off we go again.

Nice weather for Ascot. And that wicked Lester Piggott has been warned *again*. He really barges or shoves, or whatever it is he does, too often.

22 June 1969

Dear Ben,

The power of love that has made the festival so particularly moving and remarkable this year owes everything to you and Peter. You have created something wonderful and it is recognised, acknowledged and loved. The response is the evidence. I am so grateful to feel part of the affection that is the power infecting the world and the music and the sense of a very deep joy.

I have a pet quote from anon that says: 'Joy doesn't happen, it is the inevitable result of certain rules followed and laws obeyed.' Affectionate thoughts and gratitude for yet another re-creating time.

I've told Stephen Reiss I can do one or two programmes next March when I get back from Australia.

1970

The fire at Aldeburgh was caused by an electrical fault, so insurance covered the cost of rebuilding the Maltings to the original 1967 design, with improved fire precautions and bigger dressing-rooms. Even so, there were complaints about the embarrassingly visible queues for the ladies lavatories. Doris Ling, concert hall manager, put up screens to hide the queue and added a poem:

I really don't know what to do
To make life
Easier in a queue
But if you'd walk behind the screen
At least you would remain unseen.

Joyce posted another beside it:

I think that I shall never see
A more delightful WC
So clean, so fresh, so cheerful too
An absolutely lovely loo
I'm glad to raise my voice to sing
This verse in praise of Doris Ling.

The new concert hall was opened once again by the Queen and the programme included a special 70th birthday tribute to Noël Coward, arranged by Richard Rodney Bennett, and sung by Cleo Laine and Benjamin Luxon, and Joyce.

Darling Ginnie,

England at its perfect best. Suffolk is so pleasing to me; those little villages with pink and pale yellow washed houses standing in gardens with peonies bursting into ruby red and pink and white, and wisteria and laburnum drips. Chestnut trees can never have had a heavier weight of candles. And not a cloud in the sky.

Today to the Maltings to see the Queen and hear Ben conduct his concert. It is lovely to be here again. We both start beaming as we get into East Anglia and particularly in June for the Festival.

The election news is a tremendous boring thing with which we've got to live, I suppose. Wedgwood Benn's outburst against Powell is the main topic on the air today. It was violent and not at all adult. I'm allergic to both Powell and Benn because they are unappetising to look at as well as explosive. But I suppose they must be Loved! I cannot say I'm deeply concerned but it is a BORE, and if only they'd get together – Labour pool their real concern for the quality of the life we are to live and the Tories to liberate commerce but *not* allow commercial radio! I don't trust Tories, as you know! I don't trust Orrible Arold, but I do like quite a lot of the other Labours. And I think their values are more real. Enough.

Viola is staying with *very* dear people called Jean and Christopher Cowan, who have a house in Crabbe Street, Aldeburgh. She was walking very badly. Seemed to be alright but thinnish, although she says she isn't and is eating and sleeping well.

We got into our finery for the Queen and I had two or three goes before I settled on a yellow suit made of slubby linen and wore it under my Princess Alexandra's wedding coat. When was she married? I guess her son must be about seven, wouldn't you? The coat has come up lovely. No hat – 80% of people were without hats which is a sign of the times, isn't it?

The Queen looked very gay and *animated* and had on a beautiful Eton blue coat and white organza sort of beret. She sat next to Stephen Reiss who really does work full out on everything with selfless devotion. There was cheerful milling about outside with rows of children in gay cotton frocks waving flags who must have had a long wait between arrival and departure. A perfect programme lasting just an hour; Ben's realisation of 'God save the Q.' is so exacting and so terribly loving that I think everyone was ashiver with pleasure at hearing it. Also Byrd and Purcell, Mendelssohn's Scottish Symphony and Ben's sung 'Gloriana' dances. Imo Holst conducted Byrd. Imo in action is sheer delight on every level. She is unique and splendid. I dote on her for her *total* unselfconsciousness, dedication and talent and her complete honesty.

Peggy Ashcroft arrived and we sat with her in the sun for a time. She is astonishingly young-looking for 63. She's never been here before and is bowled over by the place. The feeling and the Maltings hit her between the eyes! You know how your old friend is the Universal Provider and Nanny? Peggy is wearing my extra pair of sunglasses and I've supplied her with Kleenex and cotton wool, too, all of which she'd omitted to bring with her.

Tennis next? I expect so. Tonight it is *Idomeneo*. I've had my list of rehearsals for next week and it is daily for *hours*. Bang goes the holidays. R. is very good about it. I'm sure it is needed but oh dear. All love.

Reggie joined Joan Blezard and me for Hardy poems, but Bill had never seen me in Genevieve and it followed the World Cup on telly. Bill was shattered by the match – like a small boy bewildered and bruised, and you felt he was still hoping he'd dreamed the bad news and might wake up to find Brazil hadn't beaten us after all!

Of course Peggy, looking miraculously young, read *very* well and with much intelligence. Julian Bream crouched low over his guitar didn't seem to have practised enough! And he was very restless and unaware of how disturbing it was to see him take out a large white handkerchief and wipe his strings and his hands, then return it to his pocket and start to tune, albeit silently. It was *so* irritating.

Noël's songs have *so* many tricky verses. And his ranges are really very tough. Top G down to low A flat in one song.

Cleo, in a camel-hair trouser-suit and white top, was at the Jubilee Hall, joined by Ben Luxton and our producer.

Hard work was done plotting moves and getting used to the stage. Both Ben and Cleo do their thing so beautifully. His voice is a joy to hear and if he will stop *acting* the funny numbers a little and let them happen he'll be very good. Her singing of 'City' and '20th century blues' is marvellous. This is where Richard R.B. comes into his own with ingenious jazz accompanyings, and the result of this fusion with her blues singing is very enjoyable.

Ben's voice is a joy to hear and if he will stop acting the funny numbers a little and let them happen he'll be very good.

My voice has a bit of a wheel wobble after such a long pause, for except on Sundays I haven't sung since November. It's as if the elastic is gone loose, but it usually tautens again into a better instrument and I'm singing freely up on A flat, which isn't bad for sixty.

I am learning to move and sing at the same time. Not very easy but I *can*! When in doubt I sing in Yugoslav, as Liz Welch always used to describe her gobbledy-gook in memory lapses!

Cleo is so pretty and we both like her very much. There is a quiet centre in her and a gentleness. And she is a real artist. She also loves her John Dankworth very much, and her son and daughter. He is a *charmer*. They are a most attractive pair, very dear and real. We had an interesting conversation about racialism. She is very 'realistic' about her situation and quite without any chip. She said too much fuss is made about colour and 'difference' and if it could be left alone it would happen naturally that people would get to know each other as people and that is the way to heal this separation and fear. She is actually very pale, though her hair is entirely African, but her eyes are light grey green, her mouth sensitive and wide. She is enchanting and funny and intelligent (very) and gay and warm. You'd like her. I now want to go to Ronnie Scott's in Soho and hear her and J.D. do their music. It means sitting up *so* late though.

12 June 1970

Cleo's bright magenta and scarlet all over brocade-like cotton Kaftan is becoming and gay, and my bright turquoise and emerald stands up to it well. We did two complete runs through with lights. I grow in my admiration for Cleo's work. It is so musical, so intelligent and so good. Young Ben bounces about a bit too much but he has had NO experience of this kind of thing and it is hardly fair to judge him on it. He sounds glorious. I wish he had the confidence to stand still more often.

I convulsed the company by singing a wrong word in 'Stately

homes'. The line should be: 'The baby in the Guest Wing who *crouches* in the grate (was walled up in the West Wing in 1428)', and I sang in a confident way 'The baby in the Guest Wing who *lurches* in the grate' and set them all to giggling. We finally got the sort of forbidden church or school giggles that *nothing* can stop and Colin Graham wasn't amused, but, oh dear, we were. *Agony* trying to control it. He was very patient with us.

The show was so popular that an extra midnight performance had to be arranged.

14 June 1970

Yesterday was drear and wet but we aired ourselves in the morn on a blasted heath where larks and linnets and tits were in evidence.

Cleo's singing of 'Chase me Charlie' stopped the show and justifiably. She's very gay and funny in it and adds all the sparkle it needs. Ben Luxon pulled off all his numbers wonderfully well. We had a big ovation, and I think lots of it is due to Colin Graham. Richard Rodney Bennett provided style and quality with his ingenious jazz accompanyings. Cleo's bright magenta and scarlet all over brocade-like cotton Kaftan was becoming and gay, and my bright turquoise and emerald stands up to it well.

I can see, egoist that I am, that I'd get very bored doing this sort of thing when I know what I *can* do better! But it is interesting to work with other people and good for one not to be centre at all times.

After lunch we took the car to Thorpeness Common and found a sheltered bit with gorse as windbreaks, and there we sat and read. Then we walked for hours up a pleasing cart track between fields, with a pair of splendid hares to watch, and some harebells, campion and honeysuckle to exclaim at.

In the evening the concert was glorious. Trios by Mozart, Bridge, Schubert and Beethoven, played by Yehudi, Ben and Gendron. It was *beautiful* ensemble playing. I enjoyed every note.

29 June 1970

Dear Ben

I can feel the special magic that the festival instils into music, country side, sea side and people! And it is all because Peter and you bring to it very special qualities and perception and talents and skills – and concern. Love, Joyce.

1971

Aldeburgh
7 June 1971

Darling Ginnie,

Yesterday was *so* lovely. All sunny and warm and encouraging. The rolling fields between Orford and Snape were smoky green of rising barley and all the pale plates of elderberry flowers were blooming together with the first wild roses. Enough to cause one to sing.

Last night Peter and Ben did Schubert's *Winterreise* at Snape, quite remarkably well. Those two make such a combination: considered, calm with stirrings and depths. Really something. But it is a very self-pitying wallow of a poetic cycle, isn't it? Poor little me on and on. But such music, Schubert must have been ahead of his time with this, surely?

14 June 1971

The Q. Mum in a hat made of pale pink roses came to the 3 o'clock concert, by helicopter. She sat in Ben's box and all along the edge of it were roses and green leaves – pretty. And it was a peach of a concert. The English Chamber Orchestra conducted superbly by Ben B. *Fingal's Cave* and Mozart's *Prague*. Then the interval, followed by John Ogdon and wife Brenda Lucas on two pianos rendering a romp written when he was twenty-eight by Ben on Scottish ballads and hymns. Wails of the pipes and bonny wee reels. Quite interesting. But I'm glad I'm English.

Did I tell you that there was a colossal wham two mornings ago and I thought a cupboard must have fallen over, but it was a whole yard of ceiling that dislodged itself and crumped down missing Lady Dashwood's bed by three inches! For some unaccountable reason she was not in it (8 a.m.) but had removed herself to the armchair in the only sun of the month to do her tapestry. I must say she was very good about it all.

17 June 1971

Viola is plumper and bent and her fierce little hands, so wonderfully muscular and responsive to the piano, are pale and limp and very nearly no good at all. She seems calm and restful. She is in a heavenly atmosphere of cosy, humour, warmth. Pretty things and love. Thanks be to God.

17 June 1971

At the Maltings, Heather and Janet sang duets by Tchaikovsky and Rossini and it was a delightful treat. Not important music – Victorian drawing room or concert stuff but never can it have been sing like that. Both birds in perfect voice, perfectly blended, humorous/serious, very musical and wholly enjoyable. One sat and purred. Add Ben at the piano and you really could not have surpassed the experience. He is such a superb pianist and accompanies far better than anyone else living (and is said never to practice). Brilliant and witty and warm and tender. The piano ceases to be a percussive instrument under his hands.

Max Adrian writes from Southsea where he is filming *The Boy Friend* that Ken Russell is directing and which I refused to be in. And am I glad. He says it is a long way out – 'often horrid' – and he is *not* happy. Oh dear. He says 'My silly old heart isn't enjoying the strain'. Poor Max. I think Ken Russell is sort of mad. How could he make that innocent little 'pastiche' into anything horrid I wonder? Daren't think!

Tea with Lady Barnes, widow of Sir George who founded the Third Programme when he was controller of the BBC. I felt slightly related to her because Stephen Potter and I opened the Third Programme with the 'How to Broadcast' programme. She is an intellectual, gardening type, very friendly and nice.

Lady Dashwood in a fun fur coat of horizontal stripes and very wild orange-mixed hair is to be seen. The fancy dresses and long hair and beards at the Maltings are very diverting to behold. Full peasant or Regency Buck, Gipsy or Bargee – red knotted kerchief and blue shirt open to the belly-button – take your choice.

1972

Thank you for calling. It was good to hear your voice, love. All is going well here and the lovely sense of appreciation and awareness of love that I find in Viola is very touching. She is quite helpless. Her hands lie curled in her lap. Muffet Harrison – a very nice gardening wizard – came by with a little fistful of small, perfect flowers. Wild violets, a primrose, a twig of jasmine, three pale geranium heads.

Viola read the *Guardian.* I folded it for her, pulled her legs up to lean it against, and then tried to anticipate when she was ready for a turn over. Meanwhile I dealt with a batch of sixteen letters, and in between we talked about this and that.

We saw 'Face the Music' and I looked ninety-seven and haggard. The lighting in my own shows was so careful and kind, but this fierce general lighting reveals all of the old face. I thought I was a bit down and I remember not feeling very lively when I did it.

In A Divertissement in Music and Verse, *Joyce performed with Max Adrian and the harpsichord player George Malcolm. The programme notes ran:*

> 'What, no programme notes?'
> 'Very odd, I suppose they haven't decided what to do yet.'
> 'Well, very often extempore is best, isn't it? How do you pronounce that word?'
> 'Haven't a clue. Ask Joyce, she knows all the answers. Did you see her on "Face the Music"?'

'Of course. And Max as GBS?'

'Fabulous. What a gift of the gab!'

'Will they ever stop talking and let George play, d'you think?'

'What will he play? Hummel, perhaps.'

'Himmlich, whatever it is! Lovely to have them here!'

4 June 1972

Phew! What a lot of work has gone into that programme. And of course it is worth all the slog to be able to lean on the work during the performance. I was *very* exercised about when to put on and take off me specs. It is so vital to be still when others are working. In J.C. Squire's 'The Birds' I had to cut two lines because I simply could not get through them. These are they:

'And still the thumbling *tit* and perky wren

Popped through the tiny doors of cosy *balls*'!

Max and I got hysterical giggles when I first read it, he at first pretending he hadn't heard it but having to give in when he saw the agonised look of disguised innocence on my face.

5 June 1972

We slept all afternoon and then forced ourselves up from our cocoons to bathe and dress for Ben and Peter's recital. A *beauty*. Peter sang 'The Sally Gardens' and it was meltingly lovely. Do you know *all the wheel wobble has gone* and his voice is fresh and young and of the most beautiful free quality. *All* were speaking of it. He is taking lessons all the time with a miracle teacher, he says. All I can say is: carry on. It's wonderful. He did a group of English songs by Arne, Quilter, Warlock and Tippett that I found fully pleasing. It is so restful to be allowed good tunes and gracious harmonies now and then, eh?

Later to Alfred Brendel whom I've admired on record. He proved to be a taciturn looking, long-legged feller with arms to his knees; thin; nervous and immensely gifted but too idiosyncratic for my liking. That is: he was in Haydn and Schubert, with little sudden spurts and pulling about of tempi. But in Liszt all was forgiven. It was moving and brilliant and well felt, as well as well played. A very rich afternoon.

The great thing about a holiday like this is that there *is* a lot to do and nice friends to meet with. Food here is very good. A daunting display of set piece puds.: red jelly with embedded bananas, crème caramel, and high-coloured fruit salad and arrangements of pear topped with cream cockades. Lovely fresh fish and veg. We do very well.

After lunch R. and I made for our nests like homing pigeons and zizzed under the eiders till 4. Very beneficial.

We may get a set of tennis but it's a bit moist.

11 June 1972

A gutsy afternoon of Cyril Smith and Phyllis Sellick and the Wandsworth Boys singing fit to burst. Cyril Smith's overcoming of his mammoth stroke is one of the great stories of courage. He limps on with a stick, one side wholly useless, dragged leg, hanging arm, etc. She supports him lightly, looking radiant. At the piano he hooks stick on the side of the Steinway, settles and plunges in with vigour and fingers of steel. They did a wonderful job on Ravel's *Pavane* and *La Valse*. Full blooded, flexible and highly enjoyable, it was one those rare easy-to-listen-to afternoons. Monteverdi and other early Byrds. And a *beauty* by Harris, followed by a group of Percy Grainger folk-song arrangements, with two pianos. The whole thing was open and confident and I loved it.

Last night Rostropovich should have been here but he wasn't let out of Russia. (Don't you love the way Commies talk of 'freedom' and comfortably forget there isn't any in Russia.) Instead, Ben had thought up a most lovely concert for our delight. Heavenly Mozart Quartet. Interesting *solo* clarinet work by Stravinsky, ending with Heather singing the 'Shepherd on the rock' with Ben and Thea King. *Marvellous.*

Heather Harper has lost 32 lbs and looks quite *beautiful.* She's taken to wearing a pile up of hair *à la grecque* on top of her head at the back and she holds herself regally and is every inch a Big Star – and no longer a Big Fat Star. She is thrilled about her new look, and no wonder. It's stunning. And she is singing superbly.

12 June 1972

Yesterday was the usual weather. All sorts. It was very curious because there were purple clouds all around us and it poured with rain on Lady Dashwood but here Bill got a tan on his nose.

The *Faust* (Schumann) was colossal and most wonderfully performed. A furore. Lots of old familiar faces including Lady Diana Cooper who really is so tautly stitched that it is alarming, can't smile and looks haunted. A ghost of beauty remains but it is an example of how NOT to do it. She is lovely though, and finding herself unable to hear in row O, got up in the middle and went down to an empty seat in row A, without explaining to Lord Gladwyn, who pursued her thinking she was ill!

A family have been collecting driftwood and flotsam to make a fire. Such a pretty sight at dusk – lots of young in bright jerseys and pants from five-year-olds upwards, all prancing around a great blaze with the silver sea behind them. As it grew dark they became silhouettes, delicious smell of sausages and smoke drifted gently our way.

1973

Joyce retired from the stage in 1973 after she lost the sight in one eye. But this didn't stop her continuing to lead a very busy life, including regular visits to Aldeburgh. That year Virginia Graham went with her, so she had no need to write about it. As a Christian Scientist she was never concerned about her own health, but she took an interest in others such as Britten's recent open heart surgery.

2 December 1973

My Dear Ben

I thought a great deal during your operation and I rejoice to know it was a success and that you are getting stronger.

I've had a bad eye so didn't go to Australia as planned but I am very well though a bit of a cyclop. But I've had a great deal to be grateful for and I am. I wonder if you found as I did – (of course my problem wasn't half as bad as yours) – that when I was unable to think much or pray I was able to find a sort of place of peace and the comforting realisation that my true being was entirely untouched and unchanged by what was going on in my body. This seemed to me to be a reinforcement of my certainty that one's spiritual being is the only real one!

How I enjoyed the Britten festival on radio and TV last Sunday.

With affectionate thoughts and love too to you both,

Joyce.

1974

Darling Virginia

When I got to Liverpool Street Station, after a leisurely bus ride for free on my OAP ticket, there was still forty minutes to go. I was chatting to a fan ticket collector, when there was an excitement – 'Clear the station, it's a bomb scare.' So we all went out into the street. I went up a side turning and did some praying. I thought that if there was a bomb it would be on the 6 o'clock news and R. might hear it, so I rang the Wentworth to say what had happened and that I was NOT in the station and if the bomb did go off and there wasn't a train to catch I'd ring again but otherwise to meet me as arranged. No bomb and after twenty minutes the police allowed us to go in again.

What a phlegmatic lot we *appear* to be. We all stood about in the street, some with luggage, and no one spoke! I chatted to a woman and her son about to take a train; all she had to offer was 'Tst – tst – I'm fed up with the lot of them.' The Irish, 'Them', all that make life so difficult, were embraced in that tetchy reaction.

Had a carriage to myself. Wrote a quiet, reasonable and infinitely patient complaint about the filthy condition of the Ladies at Liverpool Street Station, and sent it to the Stationmaster. My loo was full of old newspaper, a 'parcel', and general disgustingness. No towels, no soap and no attendant, though I heard her call out 'Joyce – I'm going to get a £1 worth of pennies.' Not I think addressed to me. The basins were dirty and the floor covered in papers.

I told the Stationmaster, misnamed Mr Savoury, that I knew

he had staff troubles (the usual excuse so I got it in first) but that as there was an attendant surely she should keep the place in some sort of order. What foreigners would think of it all. Definite evidence that we are third rate nation ...

Wild roses festooned the embankments as we got into the country. At Woodbridge, where the estuary is near the station, a sailing race was just starting. Dinghies. *So* pretty in the evening light – little while sails, a few red and one blue. Sea and sky the same soft harebell colour.

Reggie met me at Saxmundham and we bowled along to Aldeburgh. We will have a bite at the Maltings restaurant before hearing Peter P. and a pianist called something very like Pyorreah do Schumann . I'll just look him up for you ... Murray Perahia. Murray – Scots? Perahia – Indian? We shall see.

17 June 1974

We were greeted on all sides and my pal who marshals the cars in the car park held up everyone to grasp my hand and say 'Hello Joyce – I watch you reg'lar in "Face the Music".'

Murray Perahia is not a Scottish–Indian, he is a Jewish–Mexican, and he won the Leeds prize. He looks very young but is twenty-seven and he is a joy to hear. Long arms and huge hands and a grin like the slit in an orange. Charm and modesty and oh! the *talent*. Evidently Ben and Peter think so too. This was his first appearance as accompanist to Peter and it worked marvellously well. A formidable technique. Viola says his right hand is less good than his left but I can't say I noticed it. The programme was broadcast and she heard it with great attention. It was a lovely concert and a good start for *our* festival.

At 6 we were bidden to drinks at the Red House. Peter P., handsome and totally white-haired now, welcomed us all. Van der Posts, and various German 'regulars'. And to everyone's pleasure Ben appeared and sat on his folding shooting-stick for twenty minutes. He looks thin, bronzed, and is now beginning to have more confidence. He had been to the morning rehearsal, where he worked hard with Peter and the boy to their great joy.

Viola is much frailer. It can't go on forever. It is *very* demanding. They are all saints.

18 June 1974

Viola was much better and stronger and one could hear what she said. It is not easy for her to form the words, but she is marvellously gallant, often funny, and we had a happy time. I think she knows she is much changed and doesn't want people to see her. Last night, with her hair brushed back and lying on two cushions, she looked absolutely stunning. Those good bones and that noble nose remain wonderful, and when, as she was last night, she is calm and apparently unfussed she is *beautiful*.

We were there after dinner to see 'Face the Music'. I thought it rather a better one, did you see it? The questions were harder, which is always more fun. Viola graciously admitted to enjoying the programmes this season – she thinks we are all more settled!

Went to the 6 o'clock concert for *Dido*. It is a boring piece until the lament, but it was well done and Janet *melted* me with her singing. She is a true artist. Back hear and listened to the Berlin Philharmonic do some Brahms on the radio and was glad I hadn't paid £8.50 to hear it.

20 June 1974

The concert last night was two duos – Peter singing with Ossian Ellis harping; Ken Sillitoe fiddling with George Malcolm harpsichording. It was a successful mixture and I was very impressed with Sillitoe's violin playing. *Beautiful* sounds and a good technique. His Mozart more to his talents than his Bach but I couldn't say why. Just a feeling. Peter sang some Bach including 'Bist du bei mir' and it was difficult not to sing along too. But I *didn't*.

There were some empty seats. Is it Ben's absence or the high prices? I think the latter. Petrol is *so* high too, and it's increasingly difficult for fixed income people to stretch to concerts at £3 a seat, and operas up to £4.50.

Came back here to lunch and found R. had had a lovely morning walking on the Snape marsh. He had seen seven avocets and thirty curlew, lots of shelduck, redshank and lovely oyster-catchers.

We are divided in our views about the timing of concerts – 6.00 or 9.00. I like 6.00 because then one eats gently about 8.30 and gets to bed at a reasonable hour. R. finds taking a bath at 4.30 not to his liking. I'm happy to bath at bedtime. Peter P. likes 6.00 best. We agree that we are not night owls and are in better form before dark. I told him how I shocked my friends by *liking* matinees.

22 June 1974

Blazing morning, and I've hung R.'s underpants out on the window-sill in a way that their actual character is disguised as simply white objects out to air.

Do you know, hand on heart, Guide's honour and no toes or fingers crossed, I am actively enjoying NOT being a worker, not being in the act. No regrets, no wistful longings as I smell the 'size' backstage. Freedom. And gratitude.

Viola was argumentative – good sign and we talked about creativity and the curious number of homosexuals who are geniuses, particularly musical geniuses. We talked about the masculine qualities in certain music and had an interesting discussion on the making of programmes – the balance of ingredients, etc. She is very bright, informed and usually right about these things. I learn as I go.

23 June 1974

It is a dish-water sea today. In the middle there was a blue time.

This morning Reggie went off on his own with field glasses, and I marched to a modern concert on my own.

Modern music like modern painting is difficult and you have to accept what you can. Imogen Holst, Rodney Bennett and Britten all made appeal, but Maconchy, Ramier and an electronic assembling of noises by Bedford played on raw nerves for me and I wanted to cry 'STOP!'

I think modern music makes no sense to us *now* but is it, perhaps, like the case of Dickens and Thackeray and others being repelled by the brutality in the face of the boy Jesus in Millais' 'In the Carpenter's Shop' – that gentle, almost saccharine picture of Victorian realism? And, again, of the cacophony Victorian hearers heard in Tchaikovsky's music. All the same I still think Stockhausen is phoney and *nothing* to do with *music*. With maths and computering perhaps; a fascinating exercise for them as understands such things, but not music. Noise is not music. Music is sound.

In the evening it was sackbuts and crumphorns, under the charms of David Munrow. Ever seen him? Four feet high and cherubic, cheeks puffed out as he blows away at a variety of ancient instruments and enhances the whole thing with his verve and drive and *skills*. He presents 'Pied Piper' on the Third, it's meant for children but I always find it full of interest. Reggie and I met David when he was on 'Face the Music' last year and we took warmly to him.

The concert began very early – twelfth century – with Gershwin-type syncopations hard to sit still to.

The final concert last night was called Four Voices and Piano – Heather Harper, Janet Baker, Peter P. and John Shirley-Quirk. Songs by Haydn, Mozart and a ravishing song cycle called *Minnespiel.* Part 2 was songs from an operetta Ben wrote in American in 1941 with Auden as librettist. It's called *Paul Bunyan.* He was an American folk hero, a giant lumberjack. One felt Auden didn't really have much to work on. But there was a good duet for men about Soup'n'Beans and an amusing and intricate solo for John S.-Q. called 'The Western Union boy'. A catchy blues tune dealt with *well* by the girls, but the very Britishness of Peter and John showed through their attempts to sing it freely.

It was one of those truly gala Aldeburgh festival evenings. Milling crowds of sun-burned faces mingled with the London ones; those in the know come in middling smart casual wear. Those in the don't-know wore gloves. At the end of the *Paul Bunyan,* Peter pointed to the box and Ben stood up to take the applause. He is pin-thin and very bent but his colour is good and it was a joy for the audience to have him there. They pounded their hands and grinned their pleasure.

We were bidden up to the Artists' Bar afterwards and to my amazement there was Ben, who asked me to sit with him. So down I sat and he spoke of wishing he had more feeling of hope and faith. 'Progress is so slow.' I said I'd found marvellous support in my little trouble from the realisation that nothing fundamental changes – one is untouched by what goes on. 'Yes,' he said doubtfully, 'but I've lost confidence.' Then he said: 'I went to see Viola and her liveliness was so astonishing it really helped me.' He said something about faith and that I had it. Yes, indeed. 'I am working at it,' he said.

29 June 1974

My Dear Ben

Just a brief word to say how good it is to see you mending.

As usual, only more so, the festival had its feeling of affection, appreciation, and simplicity. I felt it strongly and I thrill in contrast to the horrors going on and the restlessness and muddle. One was able to refresh one's sense of Truth in the unchanging certainty of music. I remember feeling this in the war when I worked for Myra Hess at the Nat Gall. Music was evidence of un-changing Truth. There was a day at the time of Dunkirk when the future had no face and someone played Mozart – a quintet – and I had a sort of revelation of the intactness of that which is true. More and more I realised that real substance is something you can't touch or see or feel.

I am very grateful to you for starting the festival and infecting it with your standards and qualities.

Viola died in July 1974, after five years of illness. In the Times *obituary, Britten wrote that Viola was* 'witty and elegant, possessed of great beauty, she was at the same time an unsparingly hard worker with very exacting standards. Her mercurial sense of humour never deserted her through the last years.'

Joyce wrote to Britten:

26 July 1974

My Dear Ben

Thank you for the lovely tribute you paid to Viola in *The Times.*

The sense of joy about her persist and it isn't just personal belief that her terrible time of illness is over, it is a far more certain thing of her actual *freedom.* I sense it totally and it has been a remarkable time of *not* grieving in a self pitying way, only a substantial certainty that all is well and continuing to open up for her. I see Viola, as it were, with her back to us tall, and straight again as she was, so swift moving and free, looking towards light. She was a very dear friend for over 30 years. We worked together a lot until our careers went in different directions. She was such a talented, dedicated, difficult, rewarding, funny, generous, beautiful, demanding intellectually, companionable creature. And she loved you both with *huge* admiration too.

Bernie Dickerson told me that the only way he got through singing his Bach at the Thanksgiving service was by hearing Viola's saying to him, 'What on *earth* made you choose something so high and so difficult!'

Love Joyce

Joyce gave the first donation to the Viola Tunnard Memorial Trust which supports students at the Britten–Pears Music School.

1975

After Benjamin Britten had a stroke, Peter Pears took over more of the running of the festival.

1 May 1975

My dear Peter

If it may be an informal talk I'd love to do it – by which I meant I can do better ad libbing in this sort of occasion and I have LOTS of opinions and plenty of experiences to draw on!

Perhaps the best plan is a sort of free-association account of what can happen to a housewife/journalist when she isn't looking – my accidental entry into the profession. I went in protesting, which seems funny now.

Retirement is glorious, but doing a few occasions such as yours on Aug. 9th is enjoyable and we are doing another series of 'Face the Music' in the autumn.

Love to Ben, please, and to you and thank you for asking me. (I don't expect a fee.) Joyce.

Wentworth Hotel, Aldeburgh
13 June 1975

Darling Virginia,

What a morning. The sea is a shimmer of sequins on palest blue under a hazy sun. The Queen Mum is forcing me to put on a skirt for her concert at 3.00!

The festival is going marvellously well. Sold out most of the time and of very high quality, everyone beams and says 'Isn't it being lovely?' Lady Dashwood has gone blondey–brown. On the whole she is nicer than once she was, so let's be glad. Always up to the minute in gear: this year she's in Laura Ashley peasant-type milkmaid garments.

Presently Ben came out on Peter's arm. He is very lame – one side hardly functions – but he looks marvellously well in the face and IS working again. He moves slowly and it must be SO frustrating. Peter looking beautiful, a little tense and tired I think.

14 June 1975

The Q. Mum came in a helicopter, landed on the golf course and lunched with Ben and Peter, served by John the Wentworth head waiter. She was in splendid trim – colossal red picture hat with net and rose and upswept brim. The audience came early and stood about in the lovely sun looking marvellously varied – many ladies in LONG garments – kaftans – skirts and tops – and housecoats! There were also bare feet in sandals and gents in shirts without jackets. Many women in trousers – all neat and summery but certainly different from when we were young and in the presence of royals. Not more than a dozen or so hats and those that were seen were not this year's models.

The programme was absolutely right for a summer day – a set of five folk-tunes arranged by Ben: fresh and rustic and brief. It was Janet's performance that shone the brightest. She is in beautiful voice and her French has become perfect. She even makes French noises as well as pronouncings and it was a ravishing time.

We had a quiet evening walking on the front with the Cowans in a beautiful still evening with a fine hair-line new moon in and out of clouds and a faint smell of the sea. The beach lupins are out – lemon yellow. A pretty little tern dived over and over again in a most skilful manner.

16 June 1975

We had a GLORIOUS time with Clifford Curzon who played as ONLY he can play. For my money he is tops for musicality, understanding of what music is about and sheer felicity of sound. He makes us forget the piano is a percussive instrument and it responds as an Aeolian harp must have responded to the winds of heaven. How's that for flossy thought! Anyway he played bloody well – Schubert and Mozart – all of it sheer joy. And not too long.

Did I tell you the pleasing take of Lyn Pritt, the owner of this hotel and what he did for his friend Stephen Reiss when S.R. was summoned to Buck Palace to receive his OBE last year? Stephen was a bit worried about going to the Palace in his battered little Mini-van and Lyn said 'I'll drive you'. He rented a chauffeur's uniform and cap, put the X sign on his dashing Citroën and drove the Reisses to London for the great occasion. And MUCH enjoyed the conversation of other chauffeurs as they congregated in the Mall and talked of their employers.

17 June 1975

The skies are thick grey and the sea, though flat, is a menacing colour – old armour.

In the afternoon Bill Blezard and I attended a talk on Britten's *Death in Venice* – masterly it was – by Colin Graham. Scene by scene, musical treatment explained – links pointed out – themes shown. It was also a clear delineation of the Mann novel and the psychological sexual images and, as I felt when I first saw it, it is really a justification of homosexuality as a creative force. It's the battle between Apollo and Dionysus in which Eros – and his eroticism – are cited as the true power. There is a growing tendency around, I find, to celebrate the 'new freedom' and flaunt the 'gay'.

Lindsay Kemp's show on Sat. Night is, apparently, straight homo-wallow and it has offended a lot of people. Peter P. told me it was brilliant and original. He agreed it has longueurs but was, I thought, on the defensive about it. Someone told us the show, done in mime by Lindsay Kemp and two other transvestite fellers, was done nude in London! We were spared that, thanks be.

Colin's exposition of the opera was really quite remarkably concentrated, clear and good. I just don't like the subject – decadence, rotting flesh, the lust that is taken for love. Its such a dark story and so tragic. Peter is MARVELLOUS in it. You will find it fascinating but one emerges feeling a bit guilty – no, dirty.

Oh FRUSTRATION. STILL no letter. Goes to show that they DO hold up the 5½p ones. Too many killings in NI. It's a vile world ... but 'entirely separate'.

But oh the bliss of my bathe yesterday evening, I went in off the steeply sloping shingle and it was perfection – buoyant, fresh and WARM.

1976

Wentworth Hotel, Aldeburgh
17 June 1976

Darling Virginia

There's a new radio in our room and a new patterned carpet. John the splendid waiter has retired alas; much missed. A dear, voluble, affable, tactful rough diamond in a not absolutely pristine white jacket. But young Roger is now in a black coat and acting mighty grown-up.

An atmosphere of excitement at the Maltings for a Ben 'first' with Janet Baker singing it: *Phèdre* from a tran. by Lowell. Janet in a Greek-like bare-shouldered halter-neck in two blues looked actually handsome and sang like a RICH lark. Very exciting indeed it was, and we gave her and Ben, in his box wearing a summer linen jacket, a standing ovation. It was such vigorous, young, music; no sign of illness or any diminution of power. The very contrary. This was wonderful in itself and gave great cause for rejoicing. And we did. Janet took many calls. She has a lovely stillness as a performer, walks with her head high in no hurry. With Callas this used to be arrogance. With Janet it is simplicity.

We were made so welcome by so many regulars. Rostropovich and Galina his wife with two pretty daughters were there. They play *en famille* tonight. Marion Thorpe, in a cardi over a print frock.

18 June 1976

The shootings at Soweto are so horrifying. Despairing. What IS the future? The radio report says the hate felt by the children is a revelation to the S.A. government. What do they expect when communications explain plainly that there IS another way of life – freedom IS a right – and they aren't being allowed to find it.

We enjoyed today's recital but some of Ben's settings of Scottish songs struck me as a bit risible. No, not the settings so much as Peter's Anglo–Scots accent. Burns goes too far with lyrics about hoggies and bawk and other obscure words.

The light on the marsh was breathtaking. High tide and the reeds still green. (The rest of the country is biscuit-coloured. Today's local radio says don't flush EVERY time because of the drought.)

Because I have taken so against the *Daily Mail* we got a *SUN* to see how it works. GHASTLY. A full-frontal bust on p.3. practically life-size. Bombers.

Soon after Benjamin Britten had a heart attack in 1976, he was given a life peerage and wrote to Joyce: 'When I feel depressed I now go around murmuring "Ouch" to myself (at your suggestion) and it cheers me up a bit.' When he died later that year, Joyce wrote to Peter Pears:

Dear Peter

I write from Melbourne to send you very much love and sympathy and our affectionate thoughts. You will have had hundreds of letters because Ben was much loved, admired and treasured and I add mine to the proviso – no answer needed.

When I think of Ben I get a feeling of light and a great strength. His music is his memorial and that is evidence of all he was and this is his continuity. We are compounded of *qualities* rather than the inward and visible signs; these, I think, are what endure – we may think it is the look, touch, sound of the one we love, but I begin to realise that it is their humour, generosity, wisdom, loyalty, courage and honesty that *are* the individual. These qualities are spiritual and therefore unchanging and eternal. This is a horrible time for you and I send my love and very real sympathy.

What a marvellous contribution Ben was given to the world and all of us. I'm very grateful to have known him and as I believe I once told him (and it's still true) the highest accolade I *ever* had given to me was the invitations to play my programmes at the Festival.

With love and thoughts, Joyce. Reggie sends his too.

1977

Wentworth Hotel, Aldeburgh
16 June 1977

Darling Ginnie

Lunch at Westleton in the little pink cottage, one of a cluster, that we bought and rent to Bert and Joan Axell. It is full of clutter. Bird pictures – birds stuffed – bird books – bits of African pottery – patchwork – mats – ashtrays – and etceteras. Both are very welcoming and love the little house, so that is v.g. ... Bert has just produced a book about Minsmere for the RSPB and Reggie says it is very enjoyable. Bert has an easy way with people and made a colossal success.

We were warmly greeted with: Now you're here it's a proper festival! Incredibly, this is the most successful festival for 12 years. So far all concerts are fully booked – at vast prices and in that huge hall. The programme cover is a charming coloured photograph of Ben taken last year with a fistful of roses.

I can't tell you how exciting it was to hear this young orchestra, brought together only a few days ago from the Royal Northern Coll. of Music, the R. Acad., the R. Coll., and the Guildhall School of Music. They come to take master-classes in a summer course, and to become a band and give a concert. But that they could be SO good in a short time astonished everyone. Such freshness of approach, such vigour, clean playing of high order and the most lovely ensemble. The audience was thrilled. I kept thinking how enormously pleased Ben must be because this was evidence of a good future. The whole evening was full of affirmation and joy.

There was a good deal of emotion at Peter's first appearance, and it must have been hard for him to take, but he has an heroic quality of bearing and a great deal of faith, and it seems he came through with great dignity and calm.

Dear Imo – in a black top and ¾ skirt – danced her way through an exquisitely performed little suite of charming music, her pa's *Brook Green* suite. I like Holst, don't you?

The same staff here – some half-retired. The young son, Michael Pritt, is now in charge and doing well. We had a delicious meal of whitebait and plaice, done to a rare turn of delicacy. I am longing to write about Aldeburgh for my next book. The festivals have been such a very enjoyable part of our lives, and Ben's invitations for me to do my programmes were the highest accolade I've ever been awarded. This certainly is one of my Pleasant Places. R's too.

Bear hug from Clifford Curzon in the lounge last night. He plays tomorrow. He hates Aldeburgh, he says. Bleak, bare, hideous and snobby. I was very surprised by the vehemence!

19 June 1977

It seems that Clifford Curzon, *before* a concert, is a fiend. Nothing is right. He rages and hits out and is well known for this so that no one is upset by it. Bert, who is in charge of the Steinways, told us that the sequence of events goes like this:

'The piano is useless – appalling, old, finished.'

'The piano is getting under control.'

'The piano is the best I've ever played on.'

I thought he was a bit harder than I expected him to be in the Beethoven, but otherwise I found it clear and splendid. Brahms was lovely. Though a lot of intermezzi together seem to add up to a thick wodge of sonorous sounds.

The Schubert was as near perfection as I've ever heard it. He played it with complete understanding, passion and control. Lovely.

We took the Blezards up to the South Bar and there we found Diana Cooper. She wore a thick grey top and trews and a big black hat, with a very long black feather boa added. Quite a sight. Her eyes are still very beautiful but the pleats that have been taken in now make the exquisite mask into something sad. Must be well over 80, and nothing sits in quite the right place except those star-blue eyes.

21 June 1977
Two little fishing-boats are chugging in on the grey sea and with their yellow-jacketed men look like a Chinese picture.

R. and I took part in a Barn Dance at the Maltings – we waltzed, promenaded, and the man passed on to the next woman so it was constant changing of partners and some stomping them round at high speed. Enjoyable and very warming. We enjoyed a small bunch of ten-year-olds scrambling through the dances with the vigour of puppies – wriggling, pushing, slight fighting and a great many giggles.

1978

15 June 1978

Darling Virginia,
Murray Perahia – my favourite pianist after Clifford Curzon – has hurt his thumb from too much practising and is out of the festival. A loss.

Nice news for me – 'Face the Music' is to repeat on BBC1 and there is definitely going to be another series next year.

Incredibly we had a glorious day. It began with brilliance and then slightly hazed over but was fine and warm and sans cloud. As we drove to hear Galina Vishnevskaya and Rostropovich the skies were a threat of navy blue and a strange light turned the fields into a psychedelic green. During the concert it thundered in a dramatic way.

The concert was all Russian and very enjoyable. Easy-to-listen-to Rimsky-Korsakov, some to words of Tolstoy. Then Glinka. Then Prokoviev. I've always been a little chary of Galina's steel-strong voice but was completely won over. It was SO clear – so strong – such lovely intonation and pianissimos and she used it so flexibly.

17 June 1978

Say what you like but the world IS a better place – more varied, more unexpected. On Thursday there was a scene in the lounge of the Wentworth that would have surprised our mothers. Do you remember John, the head waiter who was there for years? He was pally but never treated anyone with less than kindness and interest from the dimmest bores to the sparkling stars. He retired two years ago and Lynn Pritt, the owner, invited him to come and stay for the weekend during the festival. Princess Peg of Hesse instantly kissed him – the rest of us followed suit. It was natural, I thought, and very pleasant. After we were seated in the middle as part of the Peg's party of ten, I noticed that John was seated at a small table with – wait for it – Lady Dashwood!

The afternoon concert was, on paper, untempting, but proved otherwise. A new piece dedicated to Ben's memory by Fricker. A bit spikey and dry but interesting and not too long. And then the 'Ode to St Cecilia' set by Ben – lovely.

When we came out we were stunned by the wonder of the night sky, there was still faint glow in the west and it paled and turned indigo as the moon rose. Romantic, poetic, and heart-expanding.

1979

Darling Virginia,

Oh what a concert last night! James Galway in a dark brown velveteen dinner jacket and with a gilded flute, and the little princess flower-like Kyung-Wha Chung and her fiddle in all-Bach programme of trios and sonatas. A true feast. Nourishment. Much bending towards each other to relish the lovely ensemble. Rocklike performances of great fluidity – just to mix the metaphors! She had on palest lilac sleeveless, and looked like a little figure on a vase. It really was a fair treat.

Have unpacked in our own familiar room – re-papered and furniture reallocated more satisfactorily. Then to Hurren to try to beat the 15% VAT before Monday.

17 June 1979

I was pretty sure that the Mozart programme yesterday would be good because, for my money, Murray Perahia is a beautiful, sensitive, strong, graceful and brilliant player. I was right. It was sheer pleasure to be in that lovely hall, full to bursting with the sort of listening that is very much part of this occasion.

Tonight's modern concert is likely to be a tester. One work is played by plucking the strings of the pianos. Henry Cowell, who writes it 'makes extensive use of hand and forearm clusters'. What, pray, are they? 'It produces new and wondrous sounds rather than any radical change in the musical language.' Zo!

There is a first performance of *Abeja Blanca*, which means White Bee. 'This music is intentionally lush and sensual … wonderfully situated with vividly evocative images and is unashamedly romantic.' Goody.

We met the singer Jan DeGaetani and her pianist husband Gilbert Kalish in the garden of the Red House this morning. Attractive middle-aged American pair. We'd gone to see an exhibition of sculpture by Elrich put out around the lawn and the morning was blessedly warm and the light beautiful on the bronzes. A splendidly bombastic cock, an aggressive goose, a nice pig trying to get over a gate. Heads of Ben and Peter, familiar to us old Aldeburgh hands.

Peter, silvery grey and apparently in form was escorting the Kalishes and we all met up in the sun.

David Hockney has a big show in the concert hall of the new music school. The hair-raising clear and sharp portrait of David Webster sitting on a tubular steel chair that has no legs, is menacing. He faces a low long table, at the far end of which is a vase full to choking with hard red tulips too closely packed. This portrait is tight and hard and ruthless.

Most of the others are lithographs of Hockney drawings, ranging from £400 to £900. There is a single courgette, painstakingly executed in waxy crayon that is an original. Asking price £4,500. He is a skilled performer and has a photographic sense of likeness. Being what he is, the pictures are mostly of men, often full frontal, and decidedly plain with an animal peasant quality. Strangely decadent and un-heart-lifting. I admired quite often but didn't rejoice.

Sunday was pretty as can be. Stalwart ladies of our vintage swim daily at 7.30 and I see them progressing over the inhospitable beach in their bathing-wraps with towels. One is a portly type in white wig, a well-to-do solo type who lived in this hotel at one time but bored her way out of a non-responsive clientele to the pub nearby, where presumably she has found congenial ears. She shops a good deal for clothes, *on dit*. Talking of which, Princess Titu – who is Princess Peg Hesse's niece – bought NINE dresses at Hurren and has caused a frisson by her lavishness.

We dined here before the song recital of contemporary music given by a lovely American mezzo, Jan DeGaetani, who has a warm and welcome voice and great sensibility and variety. She and Peter did Ben's *Abraham and Isaac*. She also sang Vaughan Williams' settings of ten Blake poems and in these she produced clear boy's notes, whereas in a rather alarming piece in Spanish she sounded rich and luscious and very feminine. We ended with a series of Charles Ives songs and these never lie easily on the ear but are quite interesting. So it was more an evening of interested than total delight – but we did enjoy it.

Golly, what a perfect morning, haze indicating heat and NO wind. Wish I had me bathers with me. We leave early tomorrow morning, and will get home for a late egg I shouldn't wonder.

In the autumn Joyce and Reggie went to stay with Jean and Christopher Cowan to sign copies of her new autobiography In Pleasant Places.

Crabbe Street, Aldeburgh
Sunday 11 November 1979

Pretty start to the day – clear and cold and blue'n'white after fierce night-time gales. Yesterday a steady trickle of old friends came to the Aldeburgh Bookshop, including dear Bert and Joan Axell. Much greeting and gladdery. Then to Hurren's to try on the green trouser-suit for our trip to Australia.

This morning we stood in the sun with the Cowans for the Armistice Day gathering by the Moot Hall for *the* most British of ceremonies – Brownies, Cubs, Sea Scouts, British Legion, Mothers' Union, many with banners were ranged around the war memorial. A civilian sergeant-major type gave orders to salute and the life-boat gun went off for the two-minute silence.

It isn't easy to keep above these aggressive attacks of pain, but Reggie is *so* tender and supporting.

Jean has the radio on. I love music drifting from another room, don't you?

This was Joyce's last visit to Aldeburgh; she died three weeks later of cancer, aged 69 years.

If I should go before the rest of you
Break not a flower nor inscribe a stone
Nor when I'm gone speak in a Sunday voice
But be the usual selves that I have known.
Weep if you must,
Parting is hell,
But life goes on,
So sing as well.

Joyce Grenfell (1940)

Further reading

Joyce and Ginnie – A Lifetime of Letters between Joyce Grenfell and Virginia Graham, edited by Janie Hampton; Hodder & Stoughton, 1997.
'A glorious affirmation of Joyce's enthusiasm, laughter and love of friends.' Christopher Matthew, *Daily Mail*.
'Lively, loving and gorgeously silly.' Maureen Lipman, *Daily Telegraph*.

Hats Off! Poems and Drawings by Joyce Grenfell; John Murray, 2000.
'Lyrical, wistful, funny and sad – full of wit and observation.' *Gifts for Girls*.

Joyce Grenfell, by Janie Hampton; John Murray, 2002; paperback 2003.
'This is undoubtedly the definitive life of Grenfell.' Geordie Grieg, *Literary Review*.
'Like her subject, Hampton is well organised, with an excellent eye for detail.' Lynne Truss, *Sunday Times*.
'An effervescent book about an effervescent lady.' Maggie Black, *The Oxford Writer*.

My Kind of Magic: A Scrapbook by Joyce Grenfell; John Murray, 2004.
'Reading this scrapbook is such a pleasure.' *Oxford Times*.
'An entrancing little book, pleasing in so many ways.' John Ward RA.

Acknowledgements

Special thanks to the Trustees of the Britten–Pears Foundation for the use of extracts from Aldeburgh Festival programmes, and letters between Benjamin Britten and Joyce Grenfell; and John Ward CBE, RA, for use of his painting.

Index

producer 48, 64
Priestley, John Boynton
  (1894–1984) British writer 26
Pritt, Lynn, owner of Wentworth
  Hotel 79
Pritt, Michael, Aldeburgh hotelier 85
Purcell Singers 28

Queen Elizabeth II 30, 32, 56–58
Queen Elizabeth the Queen Mother
  (1900–2003) 63, 78
Queen's Hall 7

Reiss, Stephen, manager of the
  Festival 55, 79
Richter, Sviatoslav (1915–97)
  Ukrainian pianist 22, 23, 37
Rimbaud, Arthur (1854–91) French
  poet 27
Rostropovich, Mstislav, Russian
  cellist 45, 46, 68, 82, 87

Savoury, Mr, Liverpool Street
  stationmaster 70
Schubert, Herr von 29
Sellick, Phyllis, British pianist 67
Shaw-Taylor, Desmond, British
  music critic 42
Shirley-Quirk, John, British
  bass–baritone 42, 75

Sillitoe, Kenneth, British violinist 72
Sitwell, Edith (1887–64) British
  writer 27
Smith, Cyril (1911–74) British
  pianist 67
St Trinian's 7

Tear, Robert, British tenor 42
Thorpe, Marion, Suffolk resident 82
Tunnard, Viola (1917–74) British
  pianist 9, 17, 21, 23, 37, 44, 53,
  57, 63, 65, 71–77

van der Post, Ingaret (1910–95)
  psychotherapist 24, 33, 46, 71
van der Post, Laurens (1906–96)
  South African writer 24, 33, 46,
  71
Vishnevskaya, Galina, Russian
  soprano 18, 80, 87

Wandsworth Boys Choir 67
Ward, Stephen (1920–63) society
  osteopath 18
Webb, Clifton (1889–1966),
  American actor 41
Williams, John, Australian guitarist
  27
Wilson, Angus (1913–91) British
  writer 30